Poetic Confessions:

Volume I

Also by
MARIA R. PALACIOS

The Female King

Karate on Wheels: A Journey of Self Discovery

Criptionary: Disability Humor & Satire

The Goddess in This Woman:
A Journal for the Woman's Soul

The Girl in This Goddess:
An Empowerment Journal
for Girls and Young Women

The Big ~~Little~~ Black Book: An Address Book
Revealing What Women Want Men to Know

Dressing Skeletons:
A Poetic Tribute to Frida Kahlo

Poetic Confessions:

Volume I

Maria R. Palacios

Atahualpa Press, Houston, TX

POETIC CONFESSIONS:
Volume I
Copyright © 2015 by Maria R. Palacios
www.facebook.com/WriterPoetGoddessOnWheels
www.GoddessOnWheels.com

Cover Art by Tara Richardson
www.TaraLee-Richardson.ArtistWebsites.com

All rights reserved. No part of this publication may be reproduced, distributed, or transmitted, in any form or by any means, without prior written permission from the author.

Library of Congress Control Number: 2015909894

FIRST EDITION

ISBN: 978-0972648363

Printed in the United States of America

"Summer Of Seventeen," 2013 Grand Prize Winner of Pen 2 Paper Creative Writing Competition, was first published in *Carve* literary magazine, Summer, 2014.

"In The Kitchen Thinking Of Sylvia Plath," was first published in the Austin International Poetry Festival anthology, *Diverse City*, 2013.

Cover Graphic Design by Laura Fiscal

Editing and Interior Design by
WeaselWorks Freelance Editing
www.facebook.com/WeaselWorks

Published by Atahualpa Press
Houston, Texas

For Vicki Mikel, my crip mentor, role model and woman friend, whose courage and passion for life taught me more than she probably realized.

Last night I thought of you and it was painful…

painful to love you again, because when I think of you it's always so raw and so real –

thorns growing between my words, my imperfections exposed and my soul desperate, knowing that no matter what, I can't hold on to you.

You slip away and leave me nothing but your name and the memory of our bodies.

— Maria R. Palacios,

"Poetic Confessions"

TABLE OF CONTENTS

Part One: Undressing Love

X-Ray	5
The Magic Of Avocados	6
For Berenice	10
Love At Sixteen	15
Loveless Love	22
Summer Of Seventeen	25
Breasts	31
Random Memories	35
White Russian Nights	39
Letter To Myself	44
Onion Rings For Barbara	49
Masturbation Monologue	56
Undressing Love	64
Giving Birth	71
For Vicki	74
Sweeping Memories	78

Part Two: Love Affair In The Kitchen

Peeling Potatoes	91
Cooking Love	94
When Olives Talk	103
When Potatoes Fall In Love	106
Sweet Surrender	111
Red Bean Soup	117
Butterflies In The Kitchen	122
Potato Tears	127
Words On The Loose	130
Love Meal	134
Whole Potatoes	138
Sweet Potato Love	144
Breaking Free	148
The Hunger Of Women	151
Untitled Poem For An Unnamed Love	156
Love Affair In The Kitchen	160
Potatoes Fully Dressed	165
In The Kitchen Thinking Of Sylvia Plath	170
Burned Rice	174
Blame The Martini	180

Part Three: A Box Full Of Men

For Charlie	187
Desire	192
Dancing With Desire	198
Poem To A Former Lover	203
Through The Lens Of Lust	213
A Box Full Of Men	218
Prayer Of A Catholic Girl Gone Bad	228
Nameless Memory	238
Poetic Confessions	243
Special Delivery	247
Memories Of April	252
Wild Mare	260
For Mat Fraser	266
Decade Of Love	275
For Mark O'Brien	281
Dance Into My Thoughts	283
Generous	288
Loving You	291

Poetic Confessions:

Volume I

By age four I knew the magic of avocados stemmed from my mother's love.

Without it, the avocado would have been just another fruit.

Its qualities wouldn't have sprouted hope between her fingers as she scooped it out of the bowl after it had been carefully mashed into dreams of walking legs and friendly feet that were unafraid of motion.

— Maria R. Palacios,

"The Magic of Avocados"

Part One: Undressing Love

X-Ray

The spinal cord has detoured,
strayed
off the tracks of normality.
Ribs
pushed to the side,
prominent curve to the right.

Time stood still
as white coats circled
my body.
Voices echoed and bounced.
X-Rays lit up on the wall
spoke my truths,
and although I was fully dressed,
I felt ...
naked.

The Magic Of Avocados

Avocados had magic
back when my mother rubbed
avocado on my legs,
spreading its green softness
over the immobile memories
left behind by
polio.

She chose the ripe ones,
the ones
with the life experience necessary
to easily venture
into a different form,
into the magic paste I wore
as I sat
in a sunny spot
for half an hour every morning.

By age four I knew
the magic of avocados
stemmed from my mother's love.
Without it,

the avocado would have been
just another fruit.
Its qualities
wouldn't have sprouted hope
between her fingers
as she scooped it out of the bowl
after it had been carefully mashed
into dreams of walking legs
and friendly feet
that were unafraid
of motion.

I knew this.
I guess deep down
I already understood
no magic could reverse
the irreversible,
but I never said this
to my mother.

I did not want her to lose
the spark in her eyes,
the light of her smile
as she squeezed magic
out of avocados each day.

Funny how some memories

are just too stubborn
to gracefully fade
into the past.
Some rest quietly
in some comfortable place
in my mind
where it hibernates
until I cut
the next
avocado.
Four decades have passed
since the last sunny morning
when I sat
with my legs embraced
by avocado magic
until it darkened
on my skin,
its lively green
gone –
gone
to where dreams go...
gone
to the
green pastures
my feet
never got to know.

Avocados had magic
back then.
I suppose they still do.
Sometimes they rest in a bowl,
their luxurious presence
bringing a salad to life.
Sometimes they sit in a basket
waiting
for the moment
when once again
they can transform,
evolve,
jump out of their skin
and become dream,
memory,
and eventually,
poem.

For Berenice

Berenice,
I remember you now
although I haven't thought of you
in over thirty years.
I guess some memories lie dormant
until something awakens them –
a splash of cool water
over sleeping thoughts
and there you are,
as if time
had never passed.

You were badass,
outspoken Latina,
thirteen
going on thirty,
with the most beautiful brown eyes
I'd ever seen.
I had just turned fourteen
in the hospital,
where we shared dreams
and scars, and the slow drip

of I.V. lines
that paralyzed time
and put minds to sleep,
along with memories of a body
that never belonged to us
but to the people in white
who patched us up,
sewing
our socially unacceptable physicality
into garments of normality,
and putting spines back in track.
The people in white
were seamstresses and engineers.
They were needles and morphine
and the taste of death
between our lips.

But even then
you were sunshine and laughter,
whisper and dreams,
as we shared secrets
of early womanhood,
the burst of "normality"
that sprung from our chests –
the magic of breasts
and all those other things
that made us feel

real.

We giggled at the thought of sex
and wondered
at the thought of love.
"Would someone ever want me?"
you would ask
in your thirteen year old voice.
"Will someone ever love
the curvature of my spine
and the silence of bones
that never learned to talk?
Will someone ever love
legs that can't walk?"
You had never been kissed,
and at fourteen,
I had been kissed once.
Only once I had been kissed.

"You will find love," I used to promise you.
I believed you would,
and I wonder
why, thirty-some years later,
you jump back into my thoughts
and take me back to your brown eyes
and your smile,
the strength we shared, hospital days,

and the chance to be
average girls
who in the midst of pain
were able to laugh –
and I have you
to thank for that.

I thank you
for the sound of laughter in my life
back when there was
nothing to really
laugh about.
You were there for me – witchy girl,
thirteen going on thirty.
Sometimes we cried together,
but not too often.
There was too much to dream about.

I hadn't thought of you
in over thirty years...
Berenice, sweet girl,
Goddess and Witch.
By now I'm sure
you have been kissed,
and I hope that somehow
my name goes back to you
like a breath of fresh air,

like a splash of cool water
in your thoughts.

"You will find love," I used to promise you.
I hope you did, my friend.
With all my heart,
I hope
you did.

Love At Sixteen

Your name was also Maria
but you were
Maria del Pilar,
like the Virgin Mary
of your native Spain.
You went by Maripi,
with an accent on the "i"
at the end of your name.

You were beauty and intellect –
keeper of my nightmares
and my dreams.
To you I confessed my sins,
and you listened
as we sat under an old tree
on Cecil Street
and dreamed
of Prince Charming.

That was the year
you had lost your leg to cancer
and I

lost my virginity.

Life brought us together as neighbors
in the small efficiency apartments where we lived,
around the corner from the Medical Center,
walking distance from the Houston Zoo.
A fortune to live there now
but then things were different.
The poor lived there back then.
We
were "the poor."

And we shared bread and late nights,
dreams and fears.
Sometimes
your fear of death was real,
even though you never said it.
I could tell
when your darkness was present,
but you knew my darkness too,
and that's how things were for us
at sixteen.

I kept your secrets safe –
your fear of death
and your phantom pain.
You kept my sins on a leash

and let them roam free
when we sat under that tree
and you lost your hair to chemotherapy
and I lost my heart
over a man.

The whole summer
we sat there and talked.
You grew dreams and hair
beneath a white bandana
and I grew breasts
beneath a shell of cast.
At sixteen
we were already women
with a past –
our own "*telenovela*"
unfolding in our lives.

So you kept my sins
along with the memory
of your leg,
and you never complained.
To you
one leg was better than none,
and me...
I had never walked,
not gracefully like you.

I had no memory of footsteps,
and you couldn't erase
the memory of yours.

You had known
the rhythm of feet,
the music of high heel shoes
on the concrete –
things I never got to know.
Did you miss that?
I never asked.
Some things, like lonesome shoes,
are better left alone.

You were part of my world
during the most painful time
in my life.
You were the rock
and the strength,
and I,
the salty ocean of tears,
broken heart and broken wing.
You helped me fly again.
"Nobody dies of love," you used to say.
You were so right.
I'm still alive,
and I have loved many times

since then.

Looking back over three decades
I still don't know
the source of your strength.
Losing a leg seemed like nothing to you.
You never got mad.
You never fell in love.
You never cried.

To you,
life was always black and white,
acceptance
and rational thought.
Your Prince Charming
was far away into your twenties.
Mine had come and gone
and broken my soul in half
at sixteen.

Thirty years is a lifetime,
and it's been a lifetime
since I last saw you.
I know all your hair grew back
and you went back to Spain
with a suitcase full of English
and an artificial leg.

You learned to walk again
and you went home...
back to your dreams.

I think of you today
and I want to go back
to my youth,
sit under that tree with you
and share stories of ghost feet and broken hearts.
I want to believe in romance
with the same intensity
and the same insanity
of sixteen.

But sixteen is far gone,
and at forty-nine
I can only write
about that time.
Love has changed
from savage flame
to steady light.
It has gone from Prince Charming
to the sound of children
in the house,
the sound of life –
things that at sixteen
I wouldn't have grasped.

I've grown so much since then...
I know you've changed too.
I'm sure you also remember
our summer of '82 –
at least
I hope you do.

Wherever you are,
thank you for your strength
and the serenity of your thoughts.
Thank you for mending
my broken heart.
Nobody dies of love.
You were so right.
Nobody
dies
of
Love.

Loveless Love

I looked into his eyes
with anguish,
wanting to find compassion
but didn't;
wanting to find love,
the spark I had seen before –
not knowing it had never been
love,
but lust.

And how does one know the difference
at seventeen?

He had said, "I love you,"
many times –
while consuming my body
and my soul,
and drinking
from my waterfall.

He had said, "I love you,"
and even though I knew better,

I made myself believe
and went on
loving him,
a man
unworthy
of my love.

Me, at seventeen,
lost in the waters
of turbulent love.

I guess I expected more
from a man twice my age.
I thought he would turn the page
and find
the real me,
but he didn't.
He just looked the other way
and left my heart
to bleed
feelings
I could never express,
while my womb was emptied
of his memory.

I looked for compassion
that day

and found none.
I looked for love
and only found
the ashes
of what could have been,
and what I should have known.

But back then,
I didn't own
my body.

Summer Of Seventeen

You taught me how to drive
and I taught you how to kiss,
although I was seventeen
and you were twenty-two.
I fell in love thinking
I was learning from you
and I was
and I did.

To me you represented
the crip independence I wanted to own,
the freedom
I wanted to have.
You were the virgin quad
who broke his neck
once upon a sunset
early in his youth.
I was the crippled girl
who at seventeen
had no virginity to give,
despite my polio years,
despite my scars

and my own personal wars
with my body.

You were the first
crip lover in my life,
the one who taught me to drive
between necking sessions,
steamed up windows,
and moments of guilt...
but you always gave in
to the temptations of my body
even if you went to church
the following Sunday,
pretending nothing happened,
attempting to forget my lips,
the meeting of our mouths,
the buttons of my blouse,
which I kept for years
after loving you.
I'm funny with love memorabilia like that.
I keep things for a long time
and then one day let go of them
as if they had never mattered.
Perhaps that's when things become
more personal and more eternal
for they only exist
in our memories.

And memories of us
I have plenty of,
like the rainy day I took off
and went to your place
instead of going to school.
We were both such fools
when it came to love,
although you swore to not love me
as much as I claimed to love
you
at the time.
I was just a girl in your life
who fell in love
with the idea of you
and with your car –
even after I drove it into a ditch –
and never really learned
to drive
without fear.

I was better
at teaching you to love
and making love on rainy days,
writing poems you read in silence
and kept folded in your bible
like the good Christian you were.

You so wanted to say no
but my cleavage learned
to swallow your name,
and your hands had memorized
the detours
of my body.

So, there I was...this
seventeen year old girl
driving you mad
and driving your car
and it's not like it was easy
for us.

Making the transfer
to the driver's seat
meant having to deal
with moving our wheelchairs
out of the car
and putting them back
creatively using our abilities,
learning
each other's ways
of moving
and trusting
a world not made to accommodate
our needs,

not able to understand
our dreams.

Driving to us meant driving
with hand controls,
to then lose control
of ourselves again,
kissing
until we swallowed each other's soul,
and then try to figure out
how to get back to where we were
so you could drive me home,
where I would lie to my mother
and you would lie to yourself,
then to your church.

I guess it was
the lying to yourself
that made us grow apart.
You chose to believe
the concept of us
wasn't meant to be,
and I guess in some ways
you were right.
But we remain friends
loving the days we shared
in our youth.

And if I could go back in time,
I would
get in your car again
and lead you
into the temptation of my lips.
I would have to go back to seventeen
to want you the same way
and to love you again
like I once did.

Our driving lessons are now
memories of seventeen
and poems growing
between my fingers
as I think
of you.

Thirty years have come and gone
since then
and thirty more might pass,
but to me
you will always be
one of my dearest memories,
one of my dearest friends,
virgin quad I perverted
without knowing.

Breasts

A cleavage to die for.
I first got it
back when thirty was old
and forty was ancient,
back when youth
felt eternal,
promising fertility –
the fertility of love,
tender blooms of womanhood
opening themselves
to life,
feeling like spring
could never end.

Yes,
breasts are
amazing,
but mine
were magical.
They were the personification
of *Woman*
as my soul struggled

to be recognized
while inhabiting
this otherwise
strange,
physical arrangement
of love –
love often imprisoned
by expectations of normality
and goals I could never meet.
No matter how hard I tried,
my feet could not learn to speak
with the same freedom
as my breasts.

My breasts were
my personal signature,
my official
Woman certification –
proof of femininity
jumping out of my chest,
my Dolly Parton side
when I say *The Girls*,
even though they have been women
for a while.

Those who have loved them
will tell you.

They craved their beauty
like a drug,
always wanting
to come back for more,
always wanting just one more time,
the pink
soft petal caress
of my roses.

My breasts have loved...
yes, they have!
Together we have loved selflessly
and constantly,
calming the thirst
of loveless lovers –
Loveless
not because I didn't love them,
but because my breasts
were all they loved
of me.

Even so,
we loved and loved,
nursing all sorts of dreams,
allowing ourselves to be emptied
and refilled...
emptied

and refilled...
until we ran out
of words.

Random Memories

I don't know what made me google you.

Over the years I claimed
to have forgotten you.
Throughout my life
I had sworn
to not love you
anymore.

But I guess in many ways
I still did,
and I still do.
Part of me always will.

The story
of loving this much
is not a chapter I can close
all at once,
although I think
you buried the memory of my name
in the archives of your youth.

So I googled you...
thirty years into the memories
of a one-sided dream.

When at eighteen,
I wanted to believe
you loved me;
I wanted to believe
the sex we shared
could lead
to the able-bodied fairytale
of being loved by you...
man of brown,
smooth,
indigenous skin,
who let me get lost
in the idea of love,
in the reality of sex,
during a time in my life
when I thought neither was meant
for me.

And I can't say that you loved me.
You never claimed to do so,
but I know you loved my mouth
and my passion,
my long wavy black hair

and my brown eyes,
the way I made you mine
in the backseat of your blue van
in a random parking lot
while spring spoke of love
and hormones spoke of sex.

I'm not sure
what I expected to find,
but when I found your obituary,
silence fell over my words...over my memories.

I wish I could have told you
that I really did love you.
I wish I could have told you
that I forgive you
for driving me to the clinic that morning
and not looking me in the eye
when the nurse asked
if that was really
what I wanted.

I went home that day
wishing
I could rewind the clock
to the first moment we met.
But even then I can't say

I wouldn't have loved you the same
as I then did.

I don't understand loss this way.
I hold on to eternity too much.
I hold on
to the early poems
next to the words of right now
and the history of loving someone
who probably never loved
me.

Part of me
refuses to believe
you're gone.

I wish I could have
one more chance
to see my reflection
in your eyes,
and dream
of a Guatemalan moon,
the "*luna de Xelahu*"
I discovered with you
in Houston, Texas.

White Russian Nights

Twenty-one years old
in the arms of a man
who loved nothing
of me –
long, wavy dark hair
concealing my scar,
big bouncy breasts
capturing
his every move,
helping him forget
the unusual body
he
was pretending
to love.

And yes, how I wanted love!
I wanted love...
the kind
that didn't leave me empty
after sex,
the kind
that didn't label me

a mistake
as the morning sun hit my face,
the kind
that wanted to stay
and make love again
with the lights on.

My White Russian nights
were nights
of nameless men
who couldn't
bring themselves to understand
who I really was.

But...
did *I*
even know,
back then?
Back when I thought
vodka and Kahlúa were my friends,
when I, too,
wanted to pretend
to be loved by somebody
who just couldn't
love
me.

Alcohol has the ability
to make us bold,
to make us love
when there is no love
to give,
when the body next to ours
speaks of truths
we are not ready for...
and the lies
we invent
as we go.

It's been years
since my last White Russian night.
I left the Kahlúa
and the sweetness aside,
kept the vodka,
and learned to drink
like Frida.

My vodka
makes love to olives
and vermouth.
It comes to life
with jalapeño juice,
making my martini dirty
in the most sensual

of ways.

I'm no longer that young girl
hurt
by unwanted love.
I am the woman who drinks
and loves,
unafraid
of it all.

That's why
although I still love it,
I don't drink Kahlúa
anymore.
I'm not the kind
to love once and forget,
but some memories are best
to just
let go.

As a drinker
and as a lover
I have grown
into somebody else.
When I fall in love,
I do so knowing
I deserve

to be loved back.
I do so willing
to let my guard down
and give
fully.

When it comes to vodka
and when it comes to men,
I want them both
passionately spiced up.
I'm sweet enough
for the two of us.

Letter To Myself

Dear Me:

I'm not quite sure how to begin this letter.
I guess it's been a while since I last wrote to you.

Somehow words feel heavy,
as if carrying the weight of our past.
Although...they do,
don't they?

Our words and our past are always part of us,
part of this constant journey,
part of the love and the loss,
the battles we fought and won,
the ones we didn't win
and the ones
we're still fighting.

We've been together through a lot
you and I.
You have been the body
and I have been the mind.

We have also been one.
We still are,
and will always be,
no matter what.

But things were not always that way.
For years I negated your existence
and the reality of who you were –
your deformed body and your deep scars.

The years we spent apart,
I was deep into metaphors,
and you,
enduring the pain –
the pain I refused to accept while you
so passively did.
I never thanked you for that, I don't think.

It took me years to know you
and a lifetime to love you.
And I do love you.

I love you, with all your so-called imperfections –
the polio legs and the small feet,
the contour of a spine
that long ago derailed from normality –

and the soft petals of a rose
that has known more thorns than most.

All the things I now love about you
are the things I used to fear.
And I remember you now
as you were back then.

Young girl of fragile body and big words.
You wore poems beneath the metal and leather
that held your legs and your dreams together
while you struggled to walk.

I pretended not to be there,
avoiding the reality of your reflection
on the windows of a shop
where girls bought short skirts and shoes
while we looked for pens and books –
things that were safe to explain
to a world that wouldn't understand
were we to buy shoes we couldn't wear
and dare to dream of such.
No. Of course not!
That would have been too much!

By then we had learned
to keep those things to ourselves.

Most people wouldn't believe
our dreams were just
like any girl's at fourteen.
It was just easier
for us to hide inside a book.

You covered the physical wounds
and I dressed the emotional ones
with words.
That is how we lived,
split in half like *The Two Fridas*.

You often wore white,
and I wore the red of your blood
in my poems.
I don't really know
how we became one,
or when or how our stanzas merged
into what we are today:
the body and soul of a poet.
Woman
who came face to face
with herself
on the nakedness of a page.

"Dear Me," I say,
and you're always there,

in every move and every breath.
I find you beneath my pen
at the stroke of every line.
Your words become mine
and you
become my words.

Because, despite years of silence,
our words grew roots on a blank sheet of paper
and that
taught us to love life
as intensely as we do.

Thank you for being YOU.
Thank you
for being
ME.

Onion Rings For Barbara

We were best friends.
Well,
we were more than that...
We could read each other's thoughts,
and the life lines
in the palms of our hands.
We were,
like some would say,
best friends.
Twenty-two
going on sixteen.
You gave me the youth
I thought I'd lost,
and rescued me
from the poems that trapped me.

You taped
pictures of nude men
behind my door,
bought me stuffed animals
and lipstick –
things best friends do.

You know.
The things we did
behind closed doors;
secrets shared,
laughter and prank calls –
the things kids do.

But at twenty-two?
No,
we were supposed to be
serious.
We were not kids
but *college kids*
still living at home,
stuck in the dysfunctional box
of traditions we despised
but lived by.

And we lived
like frogs in a pond.
Our world was small
but together
we became
the ocean.

Our friendship
was more than friendship.

It was sisterhood
and love.
It was cutting class
and going home
to your empty house
with food from Burger King
and some forbidden movie,
the silence of your living room
and the smell of onion rings
between us.

Our friendship was all that and more.
Your space became mine
and mine yours.
Cards and notes written by you
stuck to the walls of my room.
I kept you away
from the naked men
behind my door
and close to my prayers –
close to my *Virgen de Guadalupe*,
whose eyes scolded me.
I swear
they did!

But your green eyes were all I needed;
there was no other light for me.

Even after our friendship ended,
I kept a picture of you.
But twenty-some years can lose
just about anything...
so I don't have your picture
anymore.

But I have plenty of memories
of you!
Like the day you refused to go home
without me.
There was no spot for me
at your family table.
You wouldn't hear of it,
so you spent Hanukkah with me
on Christmas day –
it was one of those years
when both shared
the twenty-fifth of December.
Christmas trees and menorahs
filled the day.

You and I
drove around Houston's empty
holiday streets,
looking for an open Burger King,
but never found one.

So we sat in the cold,
dreaming of that onion ring smell
between us.

You called your parents
from a pay phone.
I called my mother.
There was no Christmas,
no Hanukkah,
no Burger King,
just us –
best friends,
soul-mates,
and more.

But even the best friendships
come to an end.
The magic ends.
Naked men get torn off walls
and tossed into the past.
The things we think
will live forever,
die.
Twenty-two becomes old,
and forty,
ancient.
But forty was far away

back then.

We just thought we were forever.
I thought we were –
even after the day
I saw the ring.

It was on April 15th,
an Easter Sunday
that year.
I woke up
to the light of your eyes
and the sparkle of diamonds
on your finger.
You got engaged
to a man I didn't think you loved.
I was happy for you – I said.
Really.
I was.
But only because
you wanted me to be.

I didn't go to your wedding.
I was afraid of weddings –
especially yours.
I was afraid of losing you.
Deep down I knew

I already had.

You never forgave me
for not being there.
I never forgave myself,
either.

But that's how friendships die.
They die with the same force they were born.
Girlfriends are forever – I used to think.
And I still do...
You're still forever,
and I think of you
every time I pass a Burger King,
and I love you again
in the warmth
of fresh onion rings.

Masturbation Monologue

I will never forget
the first time I masturbated
to orgasm...!
An accidental pleasure I discovered
when my thigh
rubbed against my clit
while crawling on the hardwood floors,
imagining the freedom
of able-bodied kids.

The pleasure shocks
sent to my body
made me want to repeat the action,
relive the feeling,
and so I started crawling,
faster and faster,
until I collapsed, exhausted,
panting like a dying dog,
heart jumping out of my chest,
fireworks between my legs,
and absolute bliss,
because at age six

I hadn't yet learned
the concept of guilt
as it related to my body.

I'm not sure I ever did.

Masturbation is a sacred ritual to me,
a gift I give to myself
freely,
refusing to accept
the taboos
often sewn to the quilt
of my cultural experience.
I choose to reject
the fear-driven assumptions
that my crip body
is unworthy or incapable
of pleasure,
and therefore, masturbation
is my communion
with love.

It is with such loving irreverence
that I ignored my mother's warning
of Hell
after she busted me masturbating
under the covers

early one morning
on some religious holiday.
And it's not like she lifted the blankets
and saw me naked playing with myself.
It was more like
the rhythmic movement of my hand
and the expression on my face –
the soft moans of orgasmic reach –
that made her pull me out of bed,
straight into the shower,
and then to the big cathedral
where the huge paintings of Hell
were supposed to tell
the story –
the story of girls like me,
bad girls,
girls who touch themselves
down there...
Yeah..., "down there."

"It's not supposed to feel good," she said.
"If it does, it comes from the devil.
Nothing like this could come from God at all."

So I went home,
and masturbated
to the image of Jesus on my wall –

a little first communion stamp
I had taped next to my bed,
and although I always looked away
when I was about to come,
this time I looked at Jesus' face,
and nothing convinced me
I had disappointed him
or hurt him or others
in any way.

I was ten then,
experienced *masturbator* for four whole years.
As I got older,
my self-sex routine was perfected,
beautifully polished by practice.
By the time I turned twelve,
my nipples had blossomed
into dreams of tomorrow
with a promise of womanhood.

I embraced my sexuality
very early in my youth
in part, I guess, because
it was the one aspect of myself
I felt I COULD control.
Doing so was my rebellion
against an able-bodied world,

ignorant, not only to my crip truths,
but also to their own
rigid, guilt-ridden definition of self
that leaves little room for healthy rituals of self-love,
which is what masturbation becomes
when we dare to love ourselves
without fear...
without shame.

I would say that masturbation
was my best teacher as a lover.
If you know how to please yourself,
chances are you'll be better equipped
to please another
body,
another soul.
The wholeness of sex begins
with loving ourselves,
for only then are we able to truly give
honestly.

And by "give" I mean
not only sharing our bodies
but the erotic secrets of our bodies...
leading a lover's hand or tongue
to the very spot
that makes you moan,

and makes you come
rivers.

By "give" I mean
teaching our lovers what we have learned,
sharing the freedom
of loving ourselves
and our unique ways
of expressing pleasure,
of addressing our needs –
the *reasonable accommodations* of life
often denied to us...often ignored.

I'm lucky, I guess –
lucky to be
such a good lover to myself,
lucky
my early experiences led me
to personal power
instead of grief.

Masturbation
was my personal salvation
in the scarcity of lovers
(in the scarcity of bodies)
willing to love me back.
It was my comfort food,

my midnight snack,
able to satisfy
my woman hunger.

I believe most women
have a rocky beginning
with sex.
We are taught to hate ourselves
and the sacred gifts
of our erogenous zones.
As women we are called whores
if we enjoy sex
and are taught to expect
"men"
to teach us how to love our female bodies,
as if men had a clue…as if they
could possibly know,
when they barely know their own
fucked up expectations of sex
and how to please
a
woman.

That's why I masturbate
without guilt.
I masturbate – without regret –
every chance I get

to be alone with myself,
letting my fingers speak
the language of my clit...
the language of my body.

With all my experience as a lover
to myself and to others,
I confess nothing compares
to the joy of masturbation.

I refuse to feel shame,
remorse,
or
any level of guilt
for enjoying myself the way I do.

What can I say?
In the end, I am always...

Finger.

Licking.

Good!

Undressing Love

I'm not sure how I got
to where I am right now.
I mean, loving this body
and loving
with this body –
this redefined version
of beauty...
beauty I share carefully.
Even when I call myself a Goddess,
and even when my words
can radiate power,
there are parts of me
I'm not ready to share
with anyone.

And I say, "ready"
because I have learned
to never say never,
because doing so
is like challenging life
to make us break that promise.

"Never!" I used to say.
Never will I show
the deep scar on my back.
Never will I share my thighs,
my narrow hips,
my curved spine,
the ragged edges of me.

This body, I thought,
couldn't speak Love.
But it does.
My body speaks Love
fluently,
although it first learned to do it
in the language
of able-bodied lovers,
sometimes
living a lie to do it –
hiding under the covers
to conceal the scars
or faking shyness,
disguising my crip side
as much as I could,
using the magic of breasts
to distract my lover's hands.
Yes,
my breasts have always been

my magic Aces,
taking lovers places
far away from my legs.

I spent years
trying to learn new tricks,
new ways
to deceive myself
and my lovers,
enchanting them with my lips,
not letting them see too much
of the way I grab my legs,
carefully lifting them up
to remove a skirt
and allow love to fit
into my well of passion.
And although I've become a daring lover,
I still use caution
with some parts of me.

I have overcome
the fear of my scars.
Lovers now caress
the silky flesh of my thighs.
They get lost between them
until their mouths smell and taste
like woman –

this woman,
this crip woman
who undresses her soul
and her body
with a lot more honesty now
than once upon her youth.

Still...
There are parts of me
I'm not willing to share,
parts of me that still fear rejection,
body parts wounded by ignorance –
ignorance that left them fragile
and unwilling to trust.
And I just will not repeat
the things said to my feet
to make them so afraid to love,
so afraid to share.
Maybe they're just too aware
of a world that reacts with fear –
fear of skinny legs
and tiny feet that can't walk.
And that's why mine will not talk
to anybody but me.
And they do talk
to me.
They speak

in their soft little girl voices.
"Do you love me?" they ask.
"Am I pretty?" they say.
"I do love you," I respond. "And you are beautiful."

I touch
the soft velvet skin
of my legs and my feet.
How delicate they are.
How innocent they are,
despite the horrors
they were forced to live,
despite the orthopedic shoes
and braces
that once imprisoned them,
and the hard cast
that made nightmares itch
and monsters crawl
under the sheets...
the memory of white coats
and indifferent hands
treating my legs as if they were
just
another example
of what a cripple looks like...

another example
of what a cripple looks like...

another example
of what a cripple
looks like...

The polio ghosts of my early years
can echo such things in my ears
when I'm about to love someone.
That's why no lover of mine
has ever touched
the sacred nudity of my legs.
No lover of mine
has ever loved
all of me.

When I undress myself,
I do so knowing
there are those who will think
I'm not complete
for not sharing my feet
with the world.
But the truth is
some truths
are meant to stay personal.
Some things are meant to be loved

privately,
for a very long time,
before we're able to trust
and really
let go.

And I AM whole.
I am complete.
My body is the reflection
of the Great Goddess as a crip.
With my unusual curves
and my immobile feet,
I know I have always been
a landscape
of Love.

Giving Birth

I used to count
fingers and toes
on every one
of my poems
as I watched them
come to life
on the page.
Then, immediately
and carefully,
I wrapped them
in the warm safety
of the copyright symbol
next to my name.

My early words
were raised cautiously,
breastfed
with a lot of love.
They were not allowed to cry
for too long.
They stayed with me
like marsupials –

safe
from criticism,
what back then I saw
as the carnivorous predator
of poetry.

The words of my youth
were fragile,
toothless,
and helpless
upon birth,
constantly needing
to be edited
and fed
so they could some day
grow into themselves
and have a voice
of their own.

And they did.
They're all grown-up
and gone.
I was left to conceive
new babies to love
and new fingers
and toes
to count, except...

I don't do that
anymore.

My poems
are born sometimes
without
any limbs at all
and they're just
as beautiful.

I have become fearless
at giving birth
to new words.
They pop out of my womb
and immediately
fend for themselves,
learn to hunt in the dark,
survive
long nights of silence,
and become women
before growing breasts
and before blood
ever speaks
of fertility.

For Vicki

You picked me up that morning
when my ex husband left
and we went to your house in Sugarland.
You always had a way of easing my mind,
reminding me
you'd already been there
and survived.

You had your own *box full of men*,
lovers and loves who had broken your heart
but made you stronger in the process.
You learned
about the thorns and the roses
and the end of fairytales
when you were left alone
to raise a son
on your own.
You, the quad who had been told
could never get pregnant
because crippled women don't have babies...
but you did.

And you were there for me
when I, too, became a mom,
teaching me
what you had learned so far
and warning me
it would not be easy.
Motherhood was painful for you.
I hope you knew you were a great mother.
I wish I would have told you that
before losing you.

And I still can't believe you're gone.
I guess because I feel you never left.
How can you possibly ever die
and leave me to finish this journey
by myself?

From you I learned
the world doesn't end
because a man leaves us
to raise children
on our own.
You taught me to romance love,
and also the power of letting go
when we really love somebody.

I remember being so heartbroken once,

desperately obsessing over a lover
who had asked me for some "space."
You made me wipe the tears off my face
as you shared the story
of your true love,
a man you had loved
since your youth.
You wanted him more than life itself,
but you were willing
to let him go
if he said no
to the calling of your heart.
You told me how you romanced his soul
with *Twelve Days of Christmas*,
reinventing the verses of this song
and sending your love to him
with pieces of yourself
but expecting nothing
in return.

He later married you,
and stayed by your side
until the day you died,
and beyond,
because I know
he will always love you.

I will always love you too,
and I hope you knew
how important you had been to so many.
I would say now you're an angel somewhere
but I know better.
I'm sure you're rolling around in heaven
claiming crip pride,
even though you can fly.

Thank you, *Vicki Voluptuous* (as you called yourself).
Thank you for being in my life.
Thank you for helping *me* soar.

Now that I think of it...
you had always had
wings.

Sweeping Memories

Right now, I don't have
a broom.
I mourn for a few days
after the loss of one.
My brooms, like some loves,
can last
a lifetime –
we have lived
through too much
to just
let go.

Some may think
I'm strange,
but any passionate being
will understand
the special love
between a woman
and a broom,
especially
if we have flown
over a full moon

to kiss the face
of a sleeping Lover.

I,
like so many others,
have danced alone
in the kitchen,
humming memories
of love
to myself.
No other partner,
no other witness
but my broom,
the same one
that has so many times
swept broken glass
and broken dreams.

No relationship
is
what is seems.
Together we have swept
fears and pain,
chewed up puppy toys,
widowed socks,
defeated G.I. Joes,
remains of fading boyhood

around the house.
We have played cat and mouse
and hide and seek
with little boys who would peak
with devilish smiles
as they look, place by place,
and I would go room by room, sweeping
as they played.

And then again,
we have been
so many times
alone,
sweeping spilled rice
and spilled words,
spilled secrets
that shatter
when they fall.
Together,
we have swept it all.
I know my floors
with the intimacy I know
my Lovers.

And sweeping
doesn't come easy
for me.

My friendship with a broom
is one of true love.
She must be perfectly connected to me.
Not every broom is the same.
Some, I'm unable to tame
no matter how much I try.
She can't be too heavy.
She can't be too light.
My crip balance can not handle
either extreme.
She has to learn
to be with me,
as I hold her
in unconventional ways,
when I must roll with her,
lifting her
from the floor.

I put her
next to my neck,
hold her with my chin
so both my arms can be free
to roll
to the next room,
the next floor space
ready to be transformed
by our presence.

Sweeping
is hard work.
It takes upper body control
and every working muscle
in my body
to make a broom dance
to my crip tune,
to a body
not meant to learn
to speak Broom
and yet,
I have become
fluent.

Adopting a new broom
is like finding
a new dance partner,
a cleaning companion,
a trustworthy associate –
able to handle the load
and responsibility,
to keep sweeping away
mistakes,
carelessness,
accidents
and bad memories,

and still be able to dance
immediately
upon request,
putting a smile on my face
while flying me back
to 1984
or even way before then.
She takes me
deep into the past,
deep into my thoughts
flying me over woman valleys
and sacred hills
and we know exactly
how it feels
to fly,
to love
in complete
and total solitude.

We
have come and gone
by the time
the first room
is done.

That's why I can't bring myself
to the coldness

of a supermarket isle
where brooms
are packed
with promises of happy floors
and happy women.
They all look the same,
like Barbies,
and I really
resent Barbie
and her prepackaged perfection
that makes little girls believe
they will never
be beautiful.

When I see brooms
all in a row,
they all speak to me
in a robotic voice,
and I can't imagine
dancing
with any of them.

I want my brooms
to already know how to love
by the time they get to me.
I want them to take me flying
the minute I touch them.

I want to find
that comfort spot
as I grab the handle
with both hands
positioning myself
for take off.

I have never named
my brooms,
but now I wish I had
so I could have a name
to remember her by
instead of just saying,
"My old broom is broken."
People would then understand
that to me
a close friend has died,
and I just have to mourn
her loss.

Every broom I have owned
has come to me
with some personal history.
Every one of them
has been
a gift of love.
So today I sit

with my dirty floor
waiting for a new broom
to land.

I often write about hunger and live on a diet of words,
and lately on a diet of you,

which keeps me in the kitchen a lot

– peeling potatoes, peeling cucumbers, apples and more –
peeling anything with a skin, including every sin I've
ever worn.

The Catholic in me sometimes stirs up guilt,
but not enough to stop me from cooking the way I cook,
from always wanting to look for you in every meal.

The truth is that what I feel
makes me want to invent new recipes of love.

— Maria R. Palacios,

"Love Meal"

Part Two: Love Affair In The Kitchen

Peeling Potatoes

She sat at the kitchen table
peeling potatoes,
peeling memories.
One in particular,
of her youth –
age eighteen to be exact.

She was at a neighbor's house.
You know...
the neighbor with the cute son,
the friendly Italian woman who could cook anything
and made her own pasta from scratch.
That night she was making dinner,
some dish that required potatoes –
little ones, big ones, heart shaped ones,
and even those that had sprouted claws,
still attempting
to hold on to life.

That night no potato was safe.
Women gathered in the kitchen
armed with peelers and small knives

that stripped potatoes of their coarse lingerie,
leaving their pale nudity exposed.

At eighteen she should have known
the intimate affair of peeling potatoes,
the way the skin unravels between the fingers
and falls in slow motion,
as if potatoes
were undressing on their own.

She should have known
by then
the feel,
the touch,
the change of texture
as each potato rotates
while knife or peeler
unveils its final form,
layer by layer,
like a first time
love affair.

But she didn't know
any of this.
She didn't know
how to peel potatoes.

"You will never get married,"
the friendly neighbor said to her.
"If by now you don't know
how to peel a potato,
you will never get married."

Twenty years
and two marriages later,
she sits at the kitchen table
peeling potatoes,
peeling memories.
There is nobody to impress.
Potatoes are nude
and this time...
she doesn't care.

Cooking Love

When I'm hungry,
I think of you.
Or maybe
it's just that I'm hungry
for you...
hungry
for the Love I cook,
slowly,
on the stove
or sometimes in the oven
or on the grill.
In every single dish
I feel
your love
filling
my senses.

I am consumed by love
when I'm in the kitchen,
even
when busy teenagers
fill

the surrounding space
with bouncing balls
and video games
and the sound of hip-hop
in the air.
I can easily sink
into this love affair
and tune the world out
to be alone
with you.

This
is the only way
I know
how to give myself
to you
and still be whole
and still
be me.
This is the only way
I can love
without breaking
any hearts,
without breaking
any rules.

I reinvent myself,

and this love,
in every bowl of soup,
in every slice of bread.
My poems wait for you,
trembling nude
over a bed
of rice.

Rice
is my daily ritual
with love.
I cook rice lovingly
but fearlessly,
boiling away
every happily ever after
that once upon a time
might have defined
the way rice
was viewed.
There is no fairytale
when I fall in love
or when I cook,
but I dare say
there is a lot
of magic.

Magic

that makes me find
heart-shaped potatoes
and tomatoes that bleed
poetry.
Magic
that makes me feel
as delicious
as the salad
on my plate,
as luscious
as the apple I just ate
(yes, the forbidden one),
while devouring
you.

And I'm not always
this aggressive
with love
or with food,
but the red apple
spoke your name
while I was trying to tame
the beast
that makes me want you,
the hunger pangs in my soul,
that loneliness
that makes me cold

when I'm missing you
the way
I have missed you
lately.

When I'm hungry,
I think of you.
But then again,
I think I'm just hungry
for you...
hungry for the fruits and vegetables
of this love...
Your heart in my hand
as I wash a red pepper,
then a green one
carefully setting them aside
along
with my fears,
and I swear to you,
there were already tears
burning my eyes
before cutting
the onion.

Sometimes
this love makes me cry
and makes me ache –

ache
with Woman yearnings
and that constant flame,
that fire
that doesn't quite go out,
keeping desires alive
even
after I'm done
cooking.

So I come back
again and again,
meal after meal,
wanting more of you,
craving
more of us
and the way we are
in the kitchen –
our sanctuary
of love
where olives learned to talk
of passion,
where rice
becomes sacred,
and potatoes undress
without shame.

Nothing
in my kitchen
will ever be
the same,
for it has become the place
where my poems make love
to you,
the space where my words rise
from the missionary position
of cooking the routine,
of making love
without love,
and memories baking
old recipes of romance
that eventually go
stale.
Until suddenly I find myself
cooking
with complete abandon,
as if I were
an experienced chef,
unafraid of knives,
unafraid
of cooking anything,
daring
with the spices
and the heat

that rises
when we're cooking
love.

You also cook Love.
I know.
Every serving of it
has a bit of me –
a hint of Maria
in your morning tea,
a dash
of Woman
sprinkled
over your toast,
my presence
in every casserole,
my name engraved
on the skin
of every
fruit.

"I think of you when I'm hungry,"
I say,
but the truth is
I'm just hungry
for you...

I am hungry
with Woman hunger –
the kind
that makes me want
to cook,
the kind
that makes me want to look
for you
and makes me find you,
in the sacredness
of my
kitchen.

When Olives Talk

I thought of you last night,
when the four olives I drowned
in a martini
spoke your name...
And it was not
the liquor talking,
believe me.
Olives
have a lot to say,
but especially
when they're inebriated
with Love.

"Beloved," you say...
"Beloved..."
as you hold
my beating heart.
And to you
my heart belongs...
As I play
with the seed of the first olive
with my tongue,

and sip you slowly
along with my drink.

I love my olives
one by one,
as if each
were a different lover.
but to you
I always return.
I come back
to the honesty of this love
that makes olives say your name
like a whisper in the wind,
like this throbbing in my veins.
How else can I possibly explain
what loving you
feels like?

I don't often drink alone,
but last night
doing so
helped me be
alone with you,
alone with the sounds of the night,
alone with the sound of my breathing,
the loudness of words
that will never be spoken,

and promises
that will never be broken
for the sake of true love.

That's why
the olives
do the talking
when I drink alone,
like my own version of Frida
and my own version of Diego.
I'm sure you understand
the complicated dynamics
of loving this much...
this way.

I find particular pleasure
in the forbidden.
It must be
the Catholic in me.
Last night
I savored sin
as I imagined it to be,
one olive
at a time.

When Potatoes Fall In Love

Potatoes lately
make me cry.
Usually onions
are responsible
for my tears
in the kitchen,
but potatoes
speak so loudly
of romance
that just holding one
between my hands
makes my heart shiver
with love.

For years I sat
at the kitchen table
peeling potatoes
with the monotony
of routine,
peeling myself away
in each one of them
until there was nothing left

of me.

The last time I peeled potatoes
in a poem,
I was lost in the past,
but really believing
I was loving
fully.
And I sat there
peeling memories,
swirls
of potato skins
falling along
with my words
in the silence
of my kitchen.

Potatoes
said nothing
back then.
They got undressed
without saying a word.
I guess
there was
nothing
to say.
We just

gave ourselves away
in every meal
while pretending
to heal
our wounds.

Now –
and I'm not sure how –
potatoes suddenly speak
of love.
They whisper, "Beloved,"
in my ear,
and say, "*Querida,*
I am holding you now."
That's when the tears
flow,
because yet again I know
what potatoes are capable of doing
to a woman's heart.
Even when we disguise pain
as art,
there are those
who will always know
the truth.

And the truth is,
potatoes speak of love

these days.
They make love to my poems,
right there
on the kitchen table,
where once upon a time,
a few years back,
I thought there was
nobody to impress
(only memories to undress),
thinking love
had settled into wisdom,
thinking romance
had gone stale,
like the usual fairy tale
that ends at midnight –
no chariot,
no magic wand.
The pumpkin was just a pumpkin
no matter what.

But now potatoes
have magic
of their own.
They are able to cook themselves
into offerings of love,
into desires
beyond

the heat of the stove,
messages written in code
able to reach a lover,
crossing borders
and frontiers –
overcoming all the fears
of loving the way I do.

Maybe that's the reason why
I can't hide what I feel.
I get overcome by love
in every potato I peel,
in every poem I write.
The kitchen comes back to life.
I guess that's the way it is...
when potatoes
fall
in love.

Sweet Surrender

I'm making hot chocolate
tonight.
I'm not sure why
since I don't really do
chocolate.
Perhaps I'm craving
the way I feel
when the smell of chocolate
sweetens
the air.

That's when I wish
I could love chocolate
like other women do,
the way their eyes light up
at the very thought of it,
the way my eyes light up
at the very thought
of you.

And loving you
can sometimes be

like
loving chocolate...
chocolate I won't drink
because its scent is enough
to fill me.
Whatever love
you're willing to give me
is enough
for me.

So I boil
two cups of water
in a small pot
while feeling this immense
longing –
longing that only you
and chocolate
can heal –
and I can so closely feel
the heat that begins to rise
right before
the water boils.

In my hands I hold
the thick chocolate block
I had unwrapped
eagerly

like a gift.
I open each one that way,
pretending to not know
what's in there,
pretending it is my first time
making chocolate,
my first time
to ever fall
in love.

Chocolate does that to me.
And I'm not saying I'm a saint
for depriving myself
of chocolate consumption.
I have sometimes had
intense love affairs
with a cup of cocoa
when I have made it
like I do
tonight...
with that same passion
that makes me write
for you.

I love you,
I guess, like I love
chocolate,

in this forbidden,
impossible,
platonic way
that makes me boil water
late at night
to make chocolate I won't drink...
just to feel close
to you.

You make my words crave
chocolate
as I drop the thick cocoa block
in the boiling water
and watch it melt.
I swear I have never felt
so much
love.

Out of the drawer
I pull out the whisk,
knowing
every time I make chocolate
I risk
getting burned
as I come face to face
with the fire of the stove
and the fire of this love

I feel
for you.

I watch the chocolate
as it begins to foam
and realize this love
has grown
more than you ever thought
it could
and I say *you* because
I
have always known,
and I
have always
loved
you.

Maybe that's why tonight
I make hot chocolate
and offer myself to you –
smooth and rich,
sweet delight of Woman
in each cup.
And I doubt you can handle
more than one,
so drink me
slowly,

savoring
each one
of my
words,
knowing
you don't have to consume me
to make me yours,
for I already
am.

Tonight
I become for you
a drinkable metaphor:
hot chocolate
for *mi Amor* –
the steam of love
kissing your face,
my Woman heat in your hands,
and my soul
in this
poem.

Red Bean Soup
(salt and pepper to taste)

I made beans today –
red bean soup
that filled the house
with love.
From the minute they were washed
and soaked overnight,
love was already in the air,
in this love affair
with a pot of beans...
and I'm not
sure what this means,
but I know
it has
everything to do
with you.

Early morning,
alone
with my coffee;
I cried
tears of joy

over the onion I cut
before moving
to a gorgeous red pepper,
then a green one.
A half of each,
along with the onion that
made me cry,
met in a hot skillet
with half a teaspoon
of olive oil
and a garlic clove,
thinly minced,
and by then I'm convinced
of the depth
of this love.
On the side I had
a celery stick
waiting patiently
to be sliced
and be romanced
into this
concoction of love
I today called
Red Bean Soup.

Love wears
the passionate red

of ripe tomatoes
and the fresh green
of jalapeños,
when the seeds
have been removed –
their hearts scraped and
all vulnerabilities
exposed –
before joining the garlic,
bell peppers and onions
that had been sautéd.

And nothing was said
when the smell of love
filled the room,
and there was no one to whom
I would confess
what cooking beans had done
to me...
the rush of desire it ignited,
the immense love I felt
while adding each ingredient
to the 1 lb of beans
that simmered on the stove
in twelve cups of water.
They puff up and swell,
knowing so well

what love does
to beans
when cooked
by a woman who loves
like I do.

I don't hold back
at all
when I cook like this,
when I love this way...
shredding a carrot
just to add color to a dish
that didn't call
for carrots,
falling in love
with somebody
who was not looking
for love.

To have you
and to not have you
makes me cook beans
as if I could devour you
in a bowl of soup,
as if the three or so hours
it takes
to declare them "ready"

were the prelude
to physical love.
I think of you
when I add the cilantro,
the celery that had been waiting,
and a single potato,
neatly peeled,
nicely cubed.
What else can one need to cook beans
with full abandon?

And with full abandon
I made love to you today,
as usual,
in the kitchen.
It all started
by the sink...
this love flowing freely
through the running water
and then through the ink
of my pen
making me cook words of love
and beans
palabras de Amor, for you...
frijoles
para ti
mi Amor.

Butterflies In The Kitchen

I love you.
I love you with
butterfly wings
and passion that swings
from one page to the next.
when your hands touch my book
of Woman,
the written manifestation
of my life.
I'm the one
who will never be
your wife
but will always be
your Love,
and I can't say lover
right now
because lovers can break up
but true love
never
ends.

People tend to confuse love

for sex
and that's the first mistake
they make
when they try to bake love
and burn the whole loaf
instead.

I confess I only eat
when I'm hungry,
no matter how big
the temptation may seem.
I know
how to satisfy myself
and I'm not ashamed to say
that I am
my best lover –
gentle
like a peaceful lake,
able to not make
a sound,
and yet intense
like a hurricane,
holding a lover's name
between my lips
while passion slips
beneath my hands.

I can go (and have gone)
months and years
without sex...
sex,
in the
traditional form,
the kind affairs are made of,
the kind
people mistake
for love.

And who can tell me I'm wrong
when I say I make love to you
right here on this poem?
And who can say this is not
a Woman
baking love on this page?
You
make my words rise
like bread, *Amor,*
when I'm kneading
love.

And I will always need
your love
because you make me burst open
like a flower,

you make me want to
break out the flour
and make tortillas by hand.
You make me feel alive
and that's why I cook and write,
wanting to be loved
by you.
In every poem
and every bowl of rice
I imagine your eyes
over my naked
words.

In the kitchen you are
with me,
and how I wish you could stay
a little longer,
hold me a bit more
after you love me,
and touch me again
the way you do,
caressing my name
up and down the spine
of my book –
The Female King side
of me,
the one who will always be

in love with love...
in love
with you.

Today is a good day
for peanut butter tacos,
huevos rancheros
and beans
to tame my hunger
and put me at ease
with the way I love.
Words simmer
on the stove
while I come back and love you
with butterfly wings
and passion that swings
when you dine
between
my pages.

Potato Tears

I come to tears
again
in the kitchen
without peeling onions.
Potatoes
can make me cry
just as easily
when I cut into them
because potatoes
always remember
your name,
and that makes me miss you
with so much longing
that I just have to
cry.

I cry
while your name rests
between my breasts
and although I know
you will always be there,
I also know

you will never
be there
just like you will never want
to ride my *Wild Mare*
when she's in heat
and in love
with you.

And what do potatoes
have to do
with any of this?
Nothing, I guess,
and that's the beauty of it.
I give myself permission
to cry
without cutting
an onion.
I give myself permission
to write
without having to explain
the randomness of my words,
the randomness
of my pain.

Just know that for you,
mi Amor,
my potatoes today

were not peeled,
my tears
were not concealed.
I guess people
are used to me crying
when I cook.
They know onions do that
to me
but they have no idea
what potatoes do –
how they make me feel,
how they make my heart
yearn for your love...
yearn
for moments alone
with you
on the sacredness
of a blank page,
where potatoes bake themselves
into poems of love
in my kitchen.

Words On The Loose

My words run free tonight,
free
like my *Wild Mare*,
even though
they're fully aware
they can only go so far
when loving from afar
on nights like this.
A moon
aching in my cleavage
along with the name of a love
whose silence
becomes open wound
in my soul.

And I've started cooking
again –
cooking
as if doing so
could make him love me
one more time,
could make him love me
like before,

but just like my *Wild Mare*,
we can never force love.
Love
must be natural.
Love
must be set free
because only then
do we truly understand
the eternity of some loves...
the eternity
of some meals.

They say time heals
every wound
but some never do.
Some
become poems that bleed,
wild horses in an open field
or butterflies between my hands.
Everything that begins
also ends.
Logic will say so
but when it comes to love,
the way I love,
and the way I cook,
makes love become
endless,

and endless
are also some wounds
of the heart.
Those of us with a live Muse
turn pain into art
and broken hearts
into eternity.

That's why
we're able
to survive
loving the way we do...
periods of silence
between poems of love,
when forever becomes
right now.
Oh how
I miss you so,
and I say it
out loud in this page,
knowing
that when my words run loose,
my Wild Muse
runs with them.

Maybe that's why
I dare to love this way,

wounded heart
on a chopping board,
exposing my naked words
before I bake them
in a batch of potatoes
like I did
once upon a dream,
once upon
a memory
of love.

Love Meal

I often write about hunger
and live
on a diet of words,
and lately
on a diet of
you,
which keeps me in the kitchen
a lot –
peeling potatoes,
peeling cucumbers,
apples,
and more –
peeling anything
with a skin,
including every sin
I've ever worn.

The Catholic in me
sometimes stirs up guilt,
but not enough to stop me
from cooking the way I cook,
from always wanting to look

for you
in every meal.
The truth is that
what I feel
makes me want to invent
new recipes
of love.

I become salad and bread
in every poem you've read
of me.
I become a bowl of soup
and that double scoop
of lust
that makes you feel like you must
save me for later,
like something to enjoy
alone,
savoring me word for word
while I claw the page,
trying to not write your name
out loud.
When I begin to melt
in your mouth
like an M&M,
I always say I'm the yellow one,
bright like the Texas' sun

that shines through my window
while I prepare or cook
the rice,
the pasta,
the naked fruit
I become
for you.

You say that I am
your kitchen muse.
You have been mine
for a while.
You found me when my kitchen was
a place of silence,
a place of sorrow.
You made love taste like food
and food taste like love.
You turned up the heat
of my stove
and made of me
a daring cook
and a fearless
poet.
For you I am both,
Amor,
a poet
and a woman

steaming words in a pot...
metaphors that get hot,
dripping desire
when I take them off the fire
and put them on a plate.

Then I imagine you again,
loving me
loving me as if I were
the most exotic meal
you've ever eaten,
the most delicious Woman
you've ever had:
Sweet Spicy Love
a la Maria,
served
over a bed
of words.

Whole Potatoes

Today potatoes
were cooked
whole,
the little red ones
that can handle it all
and give themselves
fully, –
like I do –
in the name of hunger,
in the name of love.

And my kitchen knows
love
but it also knows
the absence of it.
Silence that sticks
to the blade of a knife
while my heart bleeds metaphors,
because if Frida bleeds melons
on a canvas,
I cook potatoes in my poems.
My

page is the clean slate,
the empty plate
and canvas of my own.
My kitchen is the studio
where my words pose nude
while potatoes exude
love.

I grow potato vines
between my fingers
after I die
of love,
even when I always say
nobody ever does.
I know there are other ways
of dying.
I have been there
many times
and still return,
sprouting hope
from beneath my grave,
bursting free above the moist Earth
that has always been
my Mother.

That's how I resurrect –
take my paintbrush of words

and paint a potato poem,
then another
and another,
poems of love,
poems of pain...
Frida poems
that let me come back again
and love
as if I have never
died,
as if I have never
lived
the anguish of cooking alone
and loving like this...
learning to carefully ration
small servings of passion,
saving them
for rainy days
when the absence
of your love
can leave me
hungry.

Maybe if I could simply have you,
I might have
already
consumed you.

Maybe
potatoes wouldn't say
the things they say
when I cook them whole
like I did today.
Maybe they wouldn't understand
love
the way they do,
helping me give myself
away
to you
in every meal,
and in every poem.

I write and cook
and cook and write
as if I might
feed you
with my words alone,
as if potatoes
painted in a poem
were more like painted breasts,
able to nourish
your soul,
and satiate your thirst
with my woman
love.

And woman love
is what I am
in
the kitchen
and in your arms.
Don't think I haven't been there,
Amor,
because
I have.
I have loved you
with delirious hunger
and delicious yearning,
feeling you pulsate between my lips,
in my hands
and in my cleavage
while I cook
for you.

That's why today I cooked
potatoes whole.
I want the wholeness of you
to make me gasp
with love,
to fill me
fully
and satisfy this hunger,

this craving
that makes me want you
the way I do
and makes me love you
with a hint of forever,
because for the rest of my life
and for the rest of yours,
in every potato we see and touch,
we shall love
each other.

Sweet Potato Love

I planted sweet potatoes
in my garden
last spring
and they grew
and they climbed
all over the place
like a waterfall
of green.

And I have seen
the bare magnificence
of them,
when they fall in love
with the wind
and with the rain,
when their roots become wild
with passion,
making leaves grip
the first thing they find,
grabbing
and clawing themselves
to the ground

or desperately hugging
a trellis
as if never wanting
to let go.

I know
what that feels like.
I have been there
before.
My potato vines
speak of love.
Immense love.
Immortal love.
They ask for so little
and give
so much,
and even when I
come back
at the end of summer
with a shovel
and a man
willing to dig
their hearts out,
they still
give themselves away
with love.

A basket
full of sweet potatoes
will then sit
on my kitchen table
and tell stories
of their own.

Each sweet potato
is beautiful
and big.
It takes two hands
to handle one,
like my breasts
once upon
a "Double D"
memory.

Yes.
My potatoes
are sweet
yummy yams I dig out
with my own hands
from the womb
of my garden.
My sweet potatoes are life.
Life
that returns

with a promise
of forever.
Life
that makes us
fall in love
all over again,
with the sun
and with the rain,
even after our heart
is torn.

Breaking Free

I have been holding back,
holding back
from expressing love
every time
I think of you –
and I think of you
a lot,
probably
more than I should.

You are
my fruits and
vegetables,
my dream of trees
and the song of spring
in my olives.

So I let myself go,
completely,
floating away to you
like a message in a bottle,
a bottle I had emptied,

consuming you slowly
over almost a month
of twice a week martinis.

I have been writing for you
like a maniac,
allowing my Wild Muse to graze
on your pastures and your fields,
allowing her to feast
without feeling regret.

But, must there be
regret?
Must I always find
guilt or fault
in the act of loving?
I don't expect you
to understand
the scars
of my growing up Catholic,
the same way you don't understand
my x-rays,
and it's O.K.
Some things about me
have
no explanation.
They simply are...

that's all.

I tried to keep
the Wild Muse in the stable
but she kicked the gates down
and took off running.
This time,
no amount of guilt
could hold her back.

The Hunger Of Women

I don't understand
the awkwardness of sex;
I've been too assertive
for too long,
and too used to
simply eating
when I'm hungry.

I've treated sex
like food,
trying to cook it
with love,
even though
sometimes it burns
before satisfying
me.

There have been
nights
of me dining alone,
savoring memories
like precious leftovers

reheated
multiple times
until the whole dish
is gone.

I guess, the problem with me
is having
no regret in my eyes
when I look at a man
after he dives
into my well
of Woman.
Women
are supposed to feel shame
after loving a man,
and I regret
absolutely
nothing.
Nothing!

Not even the times
when I have loved
a body
empty of love,
when love was
my nails digging
into somebody's back,

and the, "Oh God! Oh God!" of me
becoming prayers
of lust,
moments
when a woman must
explode.

Yes, I've had moments
like those,
when my body has been close
to total strangers,
men
whose names I can't remember,
faces
that slowly faded
into the nothingness
of just sex,
the $0.99 cent menu
at McDonald's,
and super-sized,
unhealthy fries,
accompanied by all the lies
we tell ourselves
when we are hungry
for love.

The truth is,

women are hungry.
We're hungry all the time,
and we spend our lonesome nights
cooking
big meals we don't eat,
eating
big meals we don't cook,
feeling guilty
for feeling good,
feeling bad
if we dare do
what men do
or love
like men love.

They're the go-getters;
we're the sluts.
We're supposed to preserve
our virginity,
save ourselves
for just ONE man,
train our breasts to behave,
hide the womanhood
that jumps out of our cleavage,
look
but don't touch,
and starve ourselves

until we find
Mr. Right.

In the process of all that
we just lose our appetite
and unjustly so
deny ourselves
the right
to just eat
when we're hungry.

Untitled Poem For An Unnamed Love

Our hands
caress each other
despite nations between us,
despite ages
of other loves
and our own history
of wedding vows
that hold us back
from reaching further.

"I guess, it's ok to touch
when we touch with the heart,"
I tell myself
as I get
a hand full
and a mouth full
of you,
but
where do we draw the line
and call it
what it really is?

I blush at the thought
of you reading these words,
although I know
they bare themselves
for you.
I blush at the thought
of you knowing how I look
after I've been
loved –
my pages scattered
all over the place,
the spasms of love
making my words tremble
like an autumn leaf,
leaving my hair undone
and three buttons missing
from my poems.

And who's fault is it
that, like Erica Jong's,
my own fruits and vegetables
fell in love with yours
in the wrong lifetime?
Who's fault is it
that I came to you like Frida
with my split melons
bleeding

on the canvas of your life?
Who's fault is it?
And who really cares
about what goes on
between your Muse
and mine?

Isn't that
what true love stories
are about?
A full moon
like the one I saw last night
and a lover
who misses another,
knowing
it could never
be.
Isn't that the same old song
of all brokenhearted souls
who have loved
since the beginning of time
the way I'm loving *you*
right now?

Your absence
once left me wounded,
testing every aspect of me

and my resilience with love.
It is much easier to hide
behind a metaphor
because it is easier
to have part of you
than to not have you
at all.

So now when our hands touch,
breaking the rules
of distance and time,
stretching across the oceans
just to feel each other...
when that happens, I know
that if I had to do it over,
I wouldn't change anything.

Love
doesn't get
any more intense
than
this.

It really
doesn't.

Love Affair In The Kitchen

I always think of you now
when I'm in the kitchen,
undressing vegetables
and undressing my Muse,
while yearning
for your love.

And some may think
I have no shame
for the intentional
wardrobe malfunction
of my words,
the "*Full Monte*"
of my metaphors...
thoughts that so willingly
drop the robe
in front of you.

You know
my Muse wants you
with the hunger and thirst
of a Woman

who's been waiting
for too long.
And it's not your fault
that I've been so hungry.
It's not your fault
at all.

I've purposely starved myself
so I can later feast
on your words.
Call me a masochist.
Call me
whatever you want,
but know my Muse
has already had you
and loved you
in the most intimate
of ways.
I've run my fingers
up and down your back
and your chest,
loving the manly edges
of you,
every line
and every pore,
the manhood of your own Muse...
I have unzipped it all

without regret.

The physical aspect of love
is nothing
but a big lie.
Who could prove
beyond a shadow of a doubt
that I haven't
made love
to you?
Tell me who could
and why.
Tell me
if you can deny
loving me
the way I love *you*.
Tell me if you don't feel
the warmth of my mouth,
the heat of my words
when the fire crosses
the restricted borders
of the heart.

You cross
my Equatorial Line,
the imaginary boundaries
of me.

You love my East and my West,
my North and my South,
You soothe
the turmoil of an ocean
that is supposed to be Pacific
but there is no peace
until I've been loved
by you.

That
is what the kitchen is now:
A love affair
between us...
The place where my Muse is loved
with savage instinct,
with the Woman fantasy
of clearing the table
and clearing the counter
and clearing the way
to make love.
That's what you've made of my kitchen.
That's what you have made
of me.

But even
in the insanity of all this...
I still manage to deal

with potatoes,
cucumbers,
and tomatoes,
while slowly revealing
my words.
Call it crazy
but *that*
is a Muse
in love.

It doesn't matter
what's cooking on the stove;
it doesn't matter
if it burns.
The kitchen
is now the space
where I cook
for other men
while my Muse makes love
to you.

Potatoes Fully Dressed

I loved you again today
in the kitchen,
leaving this time potatoes
fully dressed,
lovingly washing each one,
holding it in my hands,
feeling the heartbeat of love
before making the first cut,
before splitting in half
its heart...
along with mine.

I seldom prepare potatoes
like this –
I mean
without the ritual
of peeling.
There's almost
an erotic feeling
to cooking potatoes
this way.

And it's not like
I haven't done it
before.
I'm as bold in the kitchen
as I am with my lovers,
but this time it means
making love fully clothed.
I know I may never be naked
with you
but in the kitchen, *Amor*,
and
in my poems,
I will always be
nude.

The real nudity between us
is the profundity of our words.
I am content loving this way,
in this
platonic and
yet so real form
so far away from the way
I give myself
to the world.

I speak to you
with my heart wide open

and my truths exposed.
You know the real me at all times
while others read
between my lines,
trying to figure me out.
I'm a complicated map
of womanhood.

But for you I am
Maria revealed
and unveiled
just as she is...
just as I am...
Incan Goddess,
Sun Worshiper,
Butterfly Whisperer,
and so much more.
For you, *Amor*,
I become poem and song,
moments that come directly
to your hands,
because everything begins
and ends
with love.

I am love that returns to you
when you thought autumn

had arrived,
when you thought love had become
the calm and quiet days
two people share.
Suddenly, there's a Wild Mare
chasing you!
Suddenly, potatoes possess
the ability to make you think
of love...

I don't know what it's like for you
nor do I ask.
I simply believe and trust
blindly
in your love,
whether or not it is
as passionate as mine
or if I simply am
reading too much
between your lines.
All I know is
that
when you cook potatoes,
you also look for a heart in each of them...
You also look for love,
and you find
mine

in every potato you cook.
And not all of them look
like hearts.
Not all of them promise love,
but in every one of them
you shall forever find
an Ave
Maria.

In The Kitchen Thinking Of Sylvia Plath

I think of you
sometimes
when I'm in the kitchen
and the rest of the house
has gone to sleep.
That's when words haunt me.
Kitchen tile comes to life.
Cabinets flap
their one winged flap.
"*Open.*
Close.
Flip.
Flap,"
they talk –
the way things talk to us poets
when we wonder
about life
and death.

I don't know
what your kitchen was like
or what things it said to you

when you decided
to no longer hear its voice.
You got tired of cabinets
and flapping wings
that never learned to fly,
and tired of the cold tile
that kissed your bare feet...
with the same coldness of death
your body left
on your kitchen floor.

I think of you
sometimes
when I'm alone
and poems cook
on the stove.
They cook slowly
while dishes talk in the sink,
their usual clickity-clatter,
the sound of plates
and silverware
gossiping
about the intimate secrets
of our mouths.

The kitchen talks lately.
It talks about you.

It wonders what sorrows,
what darkness
you lived
in those last moments
when poems brewed
on your stove
until they burned
and you inhaled the fumes
of incinerated words –
words that died
along with you
one day
in your kitchen.

My kitchen doesn't know
your darkness,
for even when in darkness,
I see light.
I seek light.
My conversations
and the poems I cook
have never been
to that side of life,
to that side of death –
a side you learned too well,
too early.

You breathe
in the pages of your diaries
and in the leaves of poems
that have grown
between your fingers,
bursting free
and finally understanding
light.

Yes,
I think of you,
and thank you for the poems
you left scattered.
Pieces I pick up,
particles of time,
your personal recipe
for death.
I take your poems
one by one,
kiss their wounds
and give them water.
They drink from my hand.
They breathe again.
They die and resurrect
in my kitchen.

Burned Rice

People say I make
the best rice in the world –
rice that makes you
fall in love
with food,
rice
that speaks
of the fields
where the dreams
of indigenous hands
harvested life
once upon a time
in this poem.

I think of you
with immense hunger...
Cat hunger.
Woman hunger.
And I dream of rice
while I dream of you...
Arroz con pollo...
Arroz con leche...

*Arroz
con savor a ti.*
Rice that has
a taste of you
like a taste
of sin
in the most delicious
of ways.

And is it wrong
for me to think of you
this way?
To say I want you
with the same honesty I say
I love you,
even when you might think
"I love you," is nothing more
than words?

Is it wrong of me
to crave
the touch
of your loving words
on the bare skin
of my "page,"
the cleavage
of my Machu Picchu

baring it all
for you?

Is it wrong of me
to cook
with the
absent mindedness
of a woman in love,
a cat on the prowl,
and thoughts that scatter
like mice?
In the end
I still burn the rice
while thinking
of you.

But see...
the thing is that
even
a quick encounter with me
(even burned rice)
is a great adventure,
an adventure
of unimaginable love –
intensity
you barely knew
existed,

especially
in a bowl
of rice.

Crackling rice it was
tonight,
dreams almost fully burned
by infinite desire.

"Eat me," I say
every time I say
I love you.
"Eat me
like a bowl of rice.
I shall wear white for you,
the white
of pillows and linen
where your body rests
while you think
of me."

I know
you think of me.
I feel you doing so.
You know I undress your soul
when you undress
your body.

I feel you
with all my heart...
with the longing
of August nights
as they drift
into September,
into the forever
of us,
through
"I love yous"
that cling to teacups
in the morning,
dripping love
the way emotions drip
after we make
love.

Rice, Amor. Rice.
And thoughts of you
is what I ate today,
rationing food
the way I ration
love,
always
feeding others first.
And I don't care
because all I really need

is an "I love you"
from you...
and a bowl of rice.

What else is there, Amor?
What else
is
there?

Blame The Martini

Blame this dirty martini
and these spicy olives
for missing you
as the sun begins
to yawn itself
into a night
so far away
from you.

I don't know what it is
or how it started,
the romancing of the olives
in my glass.
I cannot say that it is your fault,
but...
is it mine?
And do we have to
blame someone?

The Catholic in me
tends to enjoy guilt
as much as the vodka

that gets my olives drunk.
I say the olives get drunk
because I seldom do,
although my words
do get set
on fire,
making my Muse shameless
in her expressions
of love.

But even so
and even then,
I never write your name
out loud
in my journals.

Some day,
my pages will be exposed,
spread wide open
like Sylvia Plath's
and Frida's.
My most intimate scars
for all to see,
every twist of my imperfections,
words I scratched out,
poems
I chose to never share.

One day, they will all
be bare.
One day, they will all
be nude.

That's why I hold you close,
safe
in the anonymity of this love,
carefully nestling you
between my metaphors
of Woman,
warm
in the heat
of some of my secret
words,
because I no longer know
what to call
this
bittersweet layer
of forever
wrapped
around my thoughts
of you.

It becomes easy
to blame the martini
when we say things

that shouldn't be said.
The glass in front of me becomes
the "get out of jail free" card
in the games
love
tends to play.

But I don't play games
when it comes to love.
I simply come to you
like the butterflies
that return,
time after time,
to your flowers.

I come to you
disguised as four days
of laughter
and wheels that spin
into your life
like dreams...
dreams
of *manzanilla* olives
that wait for me
frozen
in the eternity
of us.

"Be bad with me tonight," I said, and I can still
remember his hands up and down my back,
my breasts pressed against his chest,
and a hug that left glitter on his jacket,
lipstick on his upper lip, and temptation in his pocket.

— Maria R. Palacios,

"Through The Lens Of Lust"

It is the memory of that hunger that makes me think of you today, although we are years away from those moments of savage abandon, when heaven was the manhood of your poem pushing deep into me,

the back and forth thrusting of raw sex
that can leave a woman satisfied or hungrier than before.

With you it was always both, and I still loved you when I decided to let you go because you wanted more.

You wanted to be my mentor and I just wanted a lover with a penis that could write poetry and yours did.

— Maria R. Palacios,

"Poem To A Former Lover"

Part Three: A Box Full Of Men

For Charlie

We were young
and free,
two worlds that came together –
fire and wind.

You,
the red headed Gringo,
me,
the feisty Latina.
I had the fire of your red hair
and you,
the shyness of a blue eyed boy
with freckles.
I loved you
from the minute I saw you.

You were afraid
of my wheels and my Spanish
and hated me for being fluent
while you struggled
in Spanish class,
and I laughed at your accent

while you
fell in love with mine.

I taught you
the lyrics to "*Eres Tu*."
You taught me to love
the wind on my face.
And you loaded me up,
wheelchair and all,
into your "Love Bug"
(your old Volkswagen Beetle),
and we traveled like sardines
singing *Eres Tu*
and Gloria Estefan.

We were young
and free
and felt invincible.
I taught you Spanish –
the bad words first
so you could conjugate
your frustrations.
You pushed my chair
down the corridor
of a college campus
while we laughed.

English,
Español,
and *Spanglish*
became the sound of our laughter
and I loved you for that.
I did.

But there was a lot more;
we both knew it.
We felt sex growing
between our metaphors,
growing like bad weeds
in the Garden of Eden,
but you were no Adam
nor was I Eve.
We both knew that too
but said nothing.

And we did nothing
but did everything.
We even did waterfalls and parks,
popcorn and movies.
We did balconies and music,
flowers and love notes.
The whole nine yards we did,
and more,
but nothing else.

We just kept singing *EresTu*
and cursing in Spanish
all semester.
I kept dreaming
of your red tongue
and your freckles,
the beast I imagined
behind your zipper,
and the Gringo accent
that rolled off your lips
when you spoke Spanish.

I loved all that about you.
You loved me too.
I know you did.
You loved
my unconditional love
and my brown eyes.
You loved
the Spanish accent
that rolled off my lips
when I spoke English.
I know you loved that
about me.
We loved each other.

And even across time

and across marriages
I have loved you and still do
just not with sex growing
between my metaphors.
I just love you,
that's all.

Sometimes
you storm out of my closet
wearing my thoughts
and my youth –
wearing my poems.

You become memory,
bilingual story,
cuento,
Prince Charming of my youth.

You are
jeans and Volkswagen Beetle,
freckles and red headed dreams,
blue eyes and Gloria Estefan,
laughter,
poem
and wind.

Desire

I wish I could say
that I feel guilt
or shame
for loving this way.
I wish I could say I blush
when I say the things I say
to you...
when I tell you how I feel
without trying to conceal
my truths;
the beauty
of loving myself,
wearing nothing but your name
and the memory of your voice
because I need nothing else
to feel you close,
to have you here.
Your love
is always near
no matter what I do.

And as quiet as I am

when I make love to you,
sometimes after a long drought
I can't help but let out
soft
little whimpers
of love
when my woman waters run
and you throb
between my breasts.
Loving this much,
with so much delicious lust,
sometimes makes me wonder
if, to those who feel shame,
I should offer some regret
or an apology
of some sort
for being so bold
when I give myself to you
and to the world,
for sharing
my imperfect body
through the lens of this love,
because
through every paragraph
and every poem,
through every night
of self-love

and through every lover,
I am always
loving...
You.

And even if I tried
to feel
any kind of regret,
guilt,
or shame,
I simply can't
because doing it
would be a lie.
I am simply unashamed
of being who I am
and loving how I love.

I have never really known
(nor do I need to know)
what you do
with the moments I give you,
the little whimpers of love
I send your way,
as if doing so
could make you want me
the way I want you.
Does it?

Do you?
It doesn't matter, my Love.
It doesn't matter.

I have enough hunger
for the two of us.
I have enough passion
to love you alone
and make myself yours
in the sacred space
of a blank sheet of paper.
That's why you find me often
in your mailbox...
my heart
still beating fast,
my poems undone,
and my words of love
still breathing hard...
the way we breathe
when
we've just been loved.

That's what you do
for me.
That's what you give
to me.
How could I ever be ashamed

of that?
Honestly,
I don't care
what some
may think of me
for loving
with the same freedom
as my Wild Mare.

I thank you
for loving her.
I thank you
for loving me...
for quietly accepting
my woman gifts –
the photographs of my cleavage,
my bare breasted dreams,
and my shameless words.
Thank you
for letting me love you, Amor.
Thank you for letting me be
mariposa de amor
on some of your pages –
yegua salvage,
who grazes
on the sacred fields
of you.

You are my 23rd Psalm –
my prayer of love,
my prayer of lust,
forbidden fruit
I eat
without feeling any guilt,
without losing
Paradise,
savoring every moment
of what others
might call sin
and I simply call
divine,
because you wine and dine
my soul.

Dancing With Desire

I had felt desperate
to feel sensual again,
to feel wanted again,
and to remember who I was
when I claimed to be
every lover's dream
and granted wishes to those
who first drank from my soul –
the nectar
of my metaphors –
before devouring my body.

I had been feeling
alone,
neglecting
to nourish my words
with a ration
of physical passion
to make me feel alive again,
to make me want to write again,
and bring me back
to being the lover I was: ❋

CripOpatra –
in some of my poems,
Woman of fire,
and words that burn memories
into the history of those
who lusted after my Muse,
although they've never had
my body.

I had even pulled names
out of my little black box
of men,
the lovers who will always have
a piece of my heart
(and some body parts)
attached to their own eternity.

But then you found me
the other day.
You found me dancing
with my arms up in the air
and my long hair loose
like the mane of my Muse,
the Wild Mare in me
in full motion,
and when I saw you
I spoke your name

and saw this look on your face
that spoke of dreams of Maria,
the Maria I used to be
when I felt sensual.

And it's not like I was dressed
for the moment.
It was more like the moment
was dressed
for me.
I would almost call it magic
but I've become
too much of a realist
in my ways of viewing life.
Sometimes I feel
like I've been living a lie
but that day, your presence
made me feel
real.

We both know there is a thin line
between the hug we shared
and the desires that flared,
as if we were
the very fire
that burned
between us that day.

I wish
what I have to say
could come from a storybook
of fairy tales
and the innocence of youth,
but my words come from experience
and from love.
You come to me like a forbidden fruit,
offering to satiate
my Woman hunger,
and though I have been feeling so lost
and so sensually alone,
I simply can't bring myself
to consume you...
not right now
and not this way.

I only cross lines
that lead me back
to being truthful,
because I don't lie
to those I love
and I don't know if I could
pretend
this would not be a lie
to one of us.

You say I'm worth the risk,
but when it comes to sex and love,
some risks are not ours to take.
That's why instead
of feeding you my body,
I feed you my words –
the naked ones you can hold on to
when you're making love
while you think of me.
It is more erotic
to love like this,
knowing
the lust we breathe for one another
is not a "zipless fuck,"
and yet it is,
for it is made
of moments like that moment,
and the sex that grows
between the lines of this poem.

And so I add your name
to my little black box of men
as another lover
I will always love...
another chapter
in the book
of Maria.

Poem To A Former Lover

I still hunger for you
once in a while.
It's like craving cigarettes
and caffeine –
things
that are not good for me –
and yet I still indulge
in the memory of you...
of us
in a hotel room,
like wild cats
loving
as if we had never loved
before.
My body next to yours
and me getting lost
in you,
clawing your chocolate skin
while I swallowed you whole.

I always devour men that way.
I swallow them whole

so they can rebirth themselves
and love again
after loving me.
My Wild Muse
is a Wild Mare,
no matter how intensely
she might love
or care
when she's in heat.
But my Wild Muse
is no longer
twenty-something.
She's closer to half a century
of love
when perhaps she should be trying
to choose
the peaceful pastures
of life
and stop running wild
when she falls in love.

But could she?
Could I stop loving
the way I loved you?
There's no "off" button
for Love
when two souls and two bodies

come together
the way ours did.
Me,
with this body that betrays
all norms and expectations
of female beauty....
You,
the intellectual
male ego
with a female Muse,
poet
whose metaphors fit
into my woman spaces
and other places
that made my own poems spread
wide open
while the sky cried
on our window...
and I cried along with it
when you left.
That was the price to pay
for loving
the forbidden.
The long nights
without your body
and sleeping alone
was the cost of having you

for a couple of hours.

You gave me
great sex
and great books.
I gave you
my humid woman zones,
the river between my thighs
and my warm lips.
My mouth
got to know you well.
My hands
got to love you fully,
but none of that was enough
to sustain us
when the winters got longer.

I was too passionate, you said,
and you became
too intellectually serious for me.
I wanted your words to fill me
like your sex,
and I wanted your sex
to grow words of love.
And I held on
for as long as I could,
pleasuring myself

to the idea of you,
because although I had devoured
your body,
the rest of you was invented
by my hunger.

It is
the memory of that hunger
that makes me think of you
today,
although we are years away
from those moments
of savage abandon,
when heaven was
the manhood of your poem
pushing deep into me,
the back and forth thrusting
of raw sex
that can leave a woman satisfied
or hungrier than before.

With you
it was always both,
and I still loved you
when I decided
to let you go
because you wanted more.

You wanted to be
my mentor
and I just wanted a lover
with a penis that could write poetry
and yours did.

Perhaps I wasn't ready
for your depth,
and I must confess
my woman hunger
has changed a lot
since loving you.
It has become less about sex
and more about love,
less about devouring a lover
and more about giving myself,
slowly,
strictly through the Muse.

And I am madly in love
right now
with the most sacred of loves,
a man whose body
I have never touched
but whose soul
understands mine so well
that I don't need sex

to satisfy my longings.
And like you,
he's an intellectual
with a female Muse,
in many ways my mentor,
and in moments of hunger
he has been my lover
without touching me.

Yes, I guess
my hunger has changed
but mainly in the way
it gets satisfied.
The fire of my hands
no longer burns the page,
no longer leaves me lonely.
Instead it has become
a steady flame lit from afar,
the sound of love over the phone,
tears and joy and tears of joy,
I love yous in my mailbox,
all the little things you and I
never really shared.

And I'm not saying
it was your fault.
Passion brought us together...

your lust
over my pink woman petals...
my lust over the maleness of you –
your manly chest,
your able-bodied hips,
your throbbing manhood,
and your lips.

You were magic and pain,
heavy rain and heavy drought.
I loved you in time of doubt
and from that I grew
the wings
with which I now fly
and become
somebody else's butterfly...
somebody else's lover.
And if I had to do it over,
I wouldn't change a thing.
And I so thank you
for letting go of me
when it was time to let go.
Thank you
for loving my body
the way you did
and mending the broken words
of my early poetry.

When I came back to you,
my poetry had grown breasts
and pubic hair
and had a torrid affair
with Love.
My words had become mature women,
and along with them
so had I.

I had solidified
my Goddess persona,
and now looking back
I know there is
no going back
to that time in our lives.
It would be too painful
to dig through the lies
we told ourselves
in order to experience
each other.
Some things
are better left to rest
in the sarcophagus
of a poem.

And even though sometimes

I still hunger for you,
my body and soul now wear
new truths –
truths that no longer fit
in the reality of us...
the way we were
and they way we have become,
as poets,
as friends,
as lovers
whose bodies became one
in the name
of Love.

Through The Lens Of Lust

I wanted him
to change his mind
but he didn't,
and even
after we hugged goodbye
one last time,
I let hope linger
and pass
through each finger
as he slipped away
from me,
away from my grip
and the warmth of my breath
whispering lust
into his ear.
"Be bad with me tonight,"
I said,
and I can still remember
his hands
up and down my back,
my breasts
pressed

against his chest,
and a hug that left glitter
on his jacket,
lipstick
on his upper lip,
and temptation
in his pocket.

I know he could imagine me
unzipping with my teeth
every one of his fantasies.
"You're such a sweet temptation,"
he said,
and his answer was no,
although his eyes
said yes.
That was enough for me,
enough
for me to add his name
to the little black box of men,
men I have loved
and will love
forever.

And yes,
I know
forever is a long time,

but so is the eternity
of a photograph,
like the ones
he has captured of me
while my words come to life
on stage
and make me feel as immortal
as Tina Modotti –
although I haven't posed nude
in a lover's studio,
nor have I had an affair
with the man whose camera lens
loses all sense
of discretion
after photographing
me.

I wanted his camera
to lose discretion that night.
I wanted him to love me
the way he loves
his photographs.
I wanted to satiate
his hunger,
make love to him and become
the exotic dish I am
when I feed myself

to a lover.

Instead we said goodbye,
time after time,
as if wishing
we could cheat the clock
out of a few more minutes
before midnight
so the dream
wouldn't turn
into a pumpkin
when the lights went out.

We were
the last ones to leave
I guess,
wanting to believe we could
hold on to the magic
and I suppose in some ways
we did.
That's why I imagine him
alone
with the silhouette
of my photographs,
alone with the idea
of Maria
in his arms.

That's why I kept his
memory raw
until it fermented
into the words I write now,
words that get me inebriated
with the same magic of that night.
And although I do wish
he would have changed
his mind,
I don't mind
that he said no,
because a Goddess knows
how to take rejection
without feeling rejected,
how to put out the fire
without killing the flame,
and move on
with her name
and her soul
still
intact.

A Box Full Of Men

*(To all the men I've loved before.
To all of them I dedicate these words.
I'm glad you came along. You blessed my life and more...
To all the men
I've loved
before.)*

Last night I dreamed that I kissed you.
I kissed you with savage desire,
wanting to drink words
out of your lips.
Our tongues found each other
like desperate beasts.
I don't recall ever kissing anybody
the way I kissed you
in that dream,
perhaps because you were
the personification of all of you,
all the men I have loved
over the years –
the ones whose bodies I caressed,
the hearts I have possessed.
I keep those in a box
along with your names,

now phallic symbols
of my past.

I think of each of you.
In my mind
I make you one;
that way I can confess my sins
to the world
and
to no one.
But you will know it's you
when you see yourself naked
on my page.
You will know it was us,
the passion or the lust
that made us whole.

And I am unashamed
of being me
as my thoughts move down the list,
my mental "Little Black Book,"
and I take a second look
when I find you,
because it was you
with me
at the airport in Seattle
when we couldn't wait

to get into each other
and made out in the parking lot
like teenagers
with hormones on the loose.
Was I in love?
Or
was I confused?
I guess I'll never know,
nor
does it matter.

I've had my own share
of *"zipless fucks"*
even before knowing
of Erica Jong
and the bite
of her words.
And you'll know it was us
in that roadside motel in Texarkana
where we drank beer, smoked weed,
and laughed at everything
until our bodies melted
into sex.
That's the closest I've been to heaven
with a man.

I also remember that January morning

waking up next to you.
Your nudity and your maleness
by my side.
That was
my Cinderella day –
your apartment in L.A.
and that Hollywood dream
in the air.
To think of you as a stranger now
seems unreal.
I can't bring myself to call you
a one night stand
even though that's what you were.
I still keep your name
in the box of those I loved
because in my own way
I did
and do.
And I also loved you
when we met
at that fancy hotel here in Houston.
I wore my hair curly
and a striped dress,
perhaps to remember that loving you
had once imprisoned me.
That night we drank wine
and I drank

from the vast ocean of your eyes.
Then we went around
looking for a cup of coffee
to kill time
while I waited for my ride
and you waited
for the song to end
and lead you
to the next dance.

Yes. I loved you then,
and I loved you again
when we froze our asses off
on the terrace of that club
and dreamed of the party life
for which we were so underdressed,
shivering in the cold of the Bay Area
as we watched others dance
into the night.

Oh, and how I loved you so
through the distant closeness of the screen,
because
in a separate box I keep
the men who love me
from afar.
They love the woman

they invent,
the lovers we will never be
but have always been,
not knowing how.
We just know our souls make love
and peace
like literary hippies
of another time,
because the poets never died
even when the music did...
and there was no Chevy
to drive to the levee,
just the literary hippies
and our dreams.

Those of you who have loved me
have truly
loved me.
You have loved me knowing
I'll never be yours.
You have loved me knowing
I'm loving someone else.
You have loved me
out loud and in silence,
between girlfriends and wives,
between moments and times
when of me you had

nothing more
than the sound of my voice,
and the only part of me you could touch
was the skin
of my words.

You have loved me, I know.
And I have loved you too.
I have loved all of you.
But as much as I have loved,
and even when my mind was gone,
a girlfriend has always known
about every one of you.
A woman friend was there for me
to pick up the pieces you left,
help me get up,
help me forget.
She has cried with me
and for me,
because behind every man I've loved
there has been a woman
I have loved even more.
A woman
who healed me
and rescued me
from myself
and from you.

Over shots of tequila we have talked
and we have laughed.
We've talked about your silky penis
and your insecurities,
about the way your smile curves to the left
when you're turned on
and about the way you moan.
The sum and substance of your life
have been slammed on the table
like a deck of cards.
You have been my Aces
many times
but I have also lost.
I have lost my heart
more than once,
and my mind
more times
than I care to admit.

"Slut!!" Some would think,
because just like the strength of women friends,
there are those who would condemn
my truths.
Sacando los cueritos al sol...
(Exposing your dirty laundry)
"How dare she admit

to having loved so many men...
so many of them...
She
must be
a
WHORE!"

But of loving you...
any of you
and all of you,
I have no regrets at all...
Just a lot of love
and the experience that has grown
into who I am today.
That's why I conjugate your memory
in the present tense
otherwise it makes no sense
to say
I love you.

I love you
with the intensity of my twenties
and with the wisdom of my forties.
You're a page in my book,
a line
in some of my
poems...

the Aces I play
when I pull your name
out of the box.

Prayer Of A Catholic Girl Gone Bad

Oh, Maria
Madonna,
Madre Mia.
I once prayed to you
for Love
and spoke straight
from my Woman heart
to yours.

I wonder
if you still
would understand
the anguish
I again feel
over the love
of a man.
I can't
begin to explain
this aching in my heart,
this hunger in my soul –
the way I learn to speak
Butterfly,

Sparrow
and Frog,
just to say
"I love you..."
The way I become
full moon
in his sleepless
nights,
wild mare painted
on a garden wall,
and cup of tea
between his hands.
Oh, Maria...
You are
Woman of Love,
but how can I
expect you to know
about these things?

You only know
wise love,
the kind
conceived without sin.
I must confess
to wanting him
the way mortal love
wants the flesh,

with shameless abandon
and surrender,
dreaming
of nights in September,
dreaming
of eternal
love...
and the silk
of my metaphors,
the way they harden
when it's cold
or when I think
of him
this way.

And I won't let
anybody tell me
that cyber loves
don't exist,
not
when I'm living like this,
waiting by a window
like a fool
for two
or three words,
depending
on what language is used

when he says,
"*te amo*."

Virgen Maria,
my Maria of Love,
I pray to you this time
not like before.
This love
is not like the ones
from many lovers ago
and many passions back
when youth
was perhaps at fault
for some things.

Not this time.
Not this way.
I never
fell in love
like this,
loving unselfishly,
and yet
wanting so much,
because I will never again
know who I am
unless I'm loving
him.

This time, *Madre Mia*,
I pray
for his love
to never end,
for him
to never bend my soul
over in pain
like so many others have.

I pray
like we pray for rain
after a long drought.
I pray
for him to not forget
to say good morning
and good night,
because that is all
I really have
of him.

You know,
Maria,
Madre mia,
that I have prayed
for him.
I have prayed

for his heart to be healed
after it broke.
I have prayed
for the light to return
after the storm,
and today,
Madre mia, I pray
he never again
goes away
leaving me lonesome
and lost
on a Houston summer day
that doesn't end
until he returns.

You know I have prayed
for him to come back
to me
and my tears never ceased
until he did.
You knew that about me
when no one else did...
until I broke down.

And I did break down,
the way women do
when we split in half,

like *The Two Fridas* we become
when we get stabbed
by silence.
That's why this time
I pray
to you,
Maria Gratia Plena
("Hail Mary,
full of grace..."),
to hear the prayers
of this Maria
full of sin.
Please help him remember
that I'm a Woman
in love
with him.
And I don't really care
if I forever have to love
in silence
and from far away.
I don't care
if our bodies never touch
the way I sometimes wish
they could.
None of that matters
any more
as long as I hear him say

Amor...
Beloved...
Querida...
while my name
lies fully naked
next
to his words of Love.

That is all
I ask of him.
But from you,
Santa Maria,
Madre de Dios,
from you I ask
for a lot more.
I ask
to let me come to you
when I feel alone –
when I need to cry.
You never ask me why.
You just let me
do it.
I ask
for you
to keep me strong
the way you have
for so long –

otherwise I couldn't live
loving the way I do,
feeling
the way I feel,
so often explaining
long silences to my Muse,
convincing her
it doesn't hurt,
letting her be tamed
by Wise Love
while burning
in my Woman Fire.

I don't know if you know much
about fire
but I thank you
for letting me talk to you
again,
Woman to Woman,
like I always do
when I fall
in love.

You keep me sane
and make me rise above
the waters that flood
my sheets,

and my metaphors,
after his words
make love
to me.
That's all
I ever ask of him
while I lean
on
You.

Nameless Memory

I found you
just months after you had died
and I now stalk your Facebook page,
scrolling up and down
the last entries you had made...
a side of you I never knew,
because you and I
had only been
carnal lovers –
the kind
that devoured each other,
feasting on the body,
ignoring
that such intense encounters
can never satisfy
the hunger of the soul.

I always stayed hungry
after loving you.
That's why I was surprised
to learn
how intellectual

and politically outspoken
you had been –
how you were
an animal lover
and advocate
for immigrant rights,
somebody
whose soul
I would have loved
beyond the passion
of the sex we shared.
I would have loved to be your friend
and engage
in philosophical conversations
over a martini
after making love.

But you and I never made love.
We just consumed each other
with physical desperation,
with animal instincts
and claws
that left
woman markings on your back
and the aftertaste of lust
between my lips.

You were
the able-bodied lover
who loved me
without loving me,
who fed my Muse
the forbidden fruit,
and we became hungry wolves –
a random love affair
that had little to do
with love.

I simply gave you
what I had to give...
my body
and my words.
I fed you my metaphors
and my womanhood,
the flowers of my youth
and the humid pleasures
of my mouth...
poems
you couldn't read out loud,
chapters of my life
that should have died with you
but didn't.

And perhaps

that's the reason why
you have found
your way back to my pages
after I poured myself over yours,
caressing the skin
of the last thoughts
you had shared,
and feeling grateful
to have seen
the kindness
and compassion
of you...
things I never knew
while only loving
your body.

Today
I honor your memory
and lovingly place your name
in the archives of my past.
And although I know
nothing will last
forever,
I hold on...
I hold on to the eternity of some things,
I hold on to the lessons,
and immortalize our moments

by keeping the fire lit
through the flame
of my poems.

Poetic Confessions

Last night I thought of you
and it was painful...
painful to love you again,
because when I think of you
it's always so raw
and so real –
thorns growing
between my words,
my imperfections exposed
and my soul desperate,
knowing that no matter what,
I can't hold on to you.
You slip away
and leave me nothing but your name
and the memory
of our bodies.

I have never loved anybody,
or any body,
the way I loved you,
even though I knew,
of me you only loved

the heat of my sex
and the excess
of my passion.

Over the years
I have learned to ration
myself and my heart,
slowly learning to love
through the vein of my art,
giving myself away
to every lover and every love
and to every soul I have loved
throughout my life.

You –
you were one of the few
who broke my soul in half
and whose memory still hurts
beneath my poems.
I went through years of silence
and years of solitude
learning to live without you,
while my words invented
able-bodied versions of myself
as if doing so could make you
fall in love
with me.

Maybe that was
my way of holding on,
my way of staying whole,
even when part of me
felt dead.

Loving you was something
that hurt so much
that even
after decades of your absence,
my heart still aches
when I feel your name
scratching the surface
of my memories.
I know you're gone,
and your wife cried
over your grave,
saying goodbye
to the man she loved
without knowing
I had loved him too.
I wonder if she knew
that I was
part of your past.

But in the end
it doesn't really matter.

Some things, I guess,
are better left alone
and in the name of love;
let them become
personal love sessions
and poetic confessions
of my soul.

Special Delivery

I have mailed myself
to lovers
before,
packed in a box that read:
FRAGILE - HANDLE WITH CARE
BREAKABLE - DO NOT BEND
OPEN IMMEDIATELY UPON ARRIVAL

I have given myself away
in pictures and postcards
stamped
with my painted lips,
and I have mailed handkerchiefs
sprayed
with my perfume.
I have sent pens
that have written love poems,
and panties I had worn
wanting to make love
to the idea
of a lover.

I have mailed myself
in care packages
that across time have held
live woman passion –
chocolate,
candles,
coffee,
my *Love Potion Number Sixty-Nine*,
a bottle of wine,
and my bare breasts –
and love letters wearing nothing
but the lingerie
of my words.

And other times I have mailed
the DNA of my Love
in a beating heart
or a locket of my hair,
inventing a love affair
the way us women do
when we love
the impossible.

And loving you
is
loving
the impossible,

but doing so
through the lens
of maturity –
the self control that keeps me
from mailing myself to you
like I have before
to so many others.

That's why my packages to you
are more like
water for chocolate...
They seldom wear your name
and are carefully wrapped
in the truth of friendship:
a cartful of Maria
and her prayers;
my woman recipes
of romance;
a quick glance
of my world –
my world of loving you
from afar –
giving myself to you
through the sacredness
of *Wise Love*
and butterflies that bless
my cleavage.

But don't get me wrong.
I still crave you
with the wild instincts
of my Fire Horse –
this mare that wants you
with savage desire,
this Muse that dreams
of you
and your hands,
this woman
who would give anything
just to be next to you,
breathing
the same air you breathe,
because being with you
is the only thing that can heal
this ache in my soul...
my empty Sundays,
this
never-ending longing,
this hunger
that just won't go
away.

I mail myself
to you

in silence,
because it is my way
of physically
loving you,
of touching you
and feeling
the skin of this love
beneath
your fingers.
And please, Amor,
forgive me.
Forgive me
for loving you so much –
so much
that I find
a way to become
a package in your mailbox
to be close to you somehow…
to be close
to you.

Memories Of April

I miss you.
I miss you
so much right now,
so much that
I can almost touch
the anguish
of once loving you
with the pain
of love
that didn't come
with a promise
of return.

Yes, I
miss you
right now,
and I say,
"right now," because
there was a time
I couldn't eat,
I couldn't sleep,
I couldn't *live*

without missing you
the way I'm missing you
right now.

And it wasn't
supposed to happen,
loving you, that is...
loving you
the way I did.
It wasn't supposed to happen.
We pinky-promised it wouldn't
as we drank
that whole bottle of wine
and melted
into the heat
of "us,"
devouring each other
like wolves,
kissing and clawing
the nakedness
of our crip bodies
together,
the silence of legs
that have never made love –
yours or mine.
Our legs
felt as virginal

as the day we were born,
although yours
did run
once upon
an able-bodied memory –
one
you can no longer
remember
and one I
have never known.

I must admit
making love to you that night
was life changing.
It made me
a more honest lover,
less afraid
of sharing myself
and my truths,
our scars
unashamed of each other
in the nude.

You marveled
at the softness of my skin,
working your hands
from my belly

to my breasts,
and we played
like cubs
only to become wolves again...
And I kissed your neck,
your face,
so very slowly moving down
to reach that line
right beneath the nipples
where for you
feeling stops.

Then I moved back up
and kissed
your lips,
making you shiver
in pleasure
as you pulled me away,
and with your exotic accent
you said:
"So ... this
is how Goddesses make love,
isn't it? You know
how to love a man."
And I just giggled
as I let my black mane
spill

over your naked chest.
Yes,
I do know
how to love
a man,
but with you,
it was a lot more than that
because there was
no "manhood" as most
would define it.

Yet,
the intimacy our bodies shared
that night
was the most intense I have ever
shared
with any man,
and we made love
again and again,
dozens of candles lit
intensifying the heat
between us,
our crip bodies
silhouetted on the wall –
nothing
has ever been
more beautiful.

With me,
Lovers and Loves
come and go,
but few pierce my soul
the way your silence did.
Loving you became
a constant ache
in my heart,
pain
often dressed up
as art
so others wouldn't know
how much I hurt,
yet, they could still see
the bleeding fruits
of my page
like a painting
of Frida.

And although
I no longer hurt
for you
like I did before,
tonight I think of you
with great longing.
I guess spring has a way

of calling your name,
the memory
of our bodies
together,
your manly hands
having a party
with my hair,
making of me
a Maria Full of Sin
as I collapsed in your arms
the way
every woman does
after she has been
well
loved.

But the memories of you now
are just that...
memories –
moments that fade
into the night
of this poem,
the smell of April
in the air,
your name burning
in every candle I light
for the rest of my life;

I will find you
in the fire of a living flame,
and every full moon in April
I shall love you again
like I once
did.

Wild Mare

"My Muse is a slut,"
I once said to you,
warning you
about the way I love –
my heart like a sponge,
absorbing Love
from many
and squeezing myself dry
of words
because I love all of them
shamelessly.

Only those
who really love me
can survive
being my lovers,
because I love
strictly through the soul,
even
when I speak of sex.
Years can go by
this way –

loving from afar
the souls of many,
dividing and splitting myself
in many parts,
nursing many loves
and many hearts –
that unless they know
the real me
would always break.
And I don't
like to break hearts,
but I can't force myself
to love just one.
I never have
and
never will.

Love can never be held
in a prison cell;
it will always find a way
to break free.
And who can possibly blame me
for loving like this
when my Muse
is a wild mare?
I'm loving intensely
right now –

intensely
and
with everything I have –
with my strong arms
and the curved spine
of my poems,
the way certain words
lean to one side
when they get tired,
the way they have to rest
every couple of hours
just to survive the day
and still have the drive
to give myself away
as a mother.
as a lover,
as a friend.

There are no loose ends
left,
and yet
memories come undone
when I love the way I love
right now
and dare to be real
about it.
When have you ever known

a woman as honest as me
when it comes to love?
For me to tell you
that I'm loving others
while I'm loving you –
only a true Goddess
could be
as bold
and able to handle
more than one Love
at a time.

Judge me
if you must,
but I must tell you,
none of the men I have loved
with all my heart
and all my soul
have ever
judged
me.
Those who have loved me
have done so
accepting me
as I am,
with the brutal honesty
of the way I love

and the *"sluttiness"* of my Muse
as she gallops away
into the night,
time after time,
until finding Love.

And Love...
Love is what fuels
my senses,
keeps me feeling alive
while existing in a body
that betrays me,
a body
intimate with pain
and memories of imperfections
that still haunt me,
parts of me that to this day
I have never shared
with any lover,
even when I'm loving
fully.

I have
the magic of Woman –
the magic
of a woman who knows
how to love

fearlessly,
and with that fire
that most
have already
forgotten,
the scent of desire
that clings to you
after making love to my name,
words
that grow like erections
on your page
when you think
of me.

"Your Muse is not a slut,"
you lovingly said to me
as you watched her go
into the open fields
away
from you.

For Mat Fraser

I saved my cleavage for you...
late in the night,
waiting
for you to arrive
from New York.

I had been dreaming
of your British accent
and the sensuality I perceived
even before
meeting you.
And I'm not sure why
I felt that way about you.
All I know is
my sixth sense
never fails me.
I smell passion
and desire
across miles and miles
like a bloodhound.

So that night I felt

especially beautiful
sleeping
on the futon
wearing
an over-sized shirt
revealing more
than usual...
but
maybe not.

We connected
like electricity
from the minute
your blue eyes
lit the night,
shining their light
upon the woman hills
I had been saving
for you.

In the morning
we had coffee
in the bread shop
downstairs.
Our intellectual sides
met
while we calmly talked

about the scent of lust
floating like smoke
in the Berkley air.

And I never thought
I would ever meet
anybody else
able to match
my
open minded,
matter of fact,
eat and get full
approach to desire...
until I met
you –
even though
the intimacy we shared
did not involve sex
at all.

We used
our energy artistically,
transformed it
into friendship
and love,
and although
neither one of us

would ever deny
the attraction
we felt
and feel,
we just knew
it wasn't the right time
to let sex run free
into each other's
bodies.

For twelve days straight,
we took turns
buying coffee.
You never found
my morning cheerfulness
amusing
until after you'd had
caffeine.

Day after day,
I got to know your Muse.
You got to know mine.
And I remember you
rolling dreams
with your
four-finger hands
and making "hand" become

the most beautiful,
four letter word
in the dictionary.

You did amazing things
with those four-finger hands,
like lighting cigarettes
and lighting the night
in a single move,
amazing things
like massaging my shoulders
with your strange bony elbows
better than anybody
with full limbs.
Yes, I saw you do
amazing things.

Then we would sit
in the room
with the radio on
emailing each other
from across the couch.
I sent you my black cat
and my poems.
You sent me new friends
and British crip sites,
the "Ouch" of you,

and your own version
of Beauty and The Beast.
You
as the Beast.

Do you remember the times –
of course you do –
when we escaped across the street
to the haven
of vegetarian Thai food –
the magic of tofu
and brown rice
for which you paid extra
because I wouldn't eat
without it?
"You eat like a bird."

You laughed
as you dipped a piece
of fried zucchini
into my peanut sauce
while I watched in awe
the way you do everything,
as if not having thumbs
was as natural
as having them,
but for you

it is
as it is natural
for me
not to walk.

Yes,
our sharing was superb
like the many times
we sat on the roof
burning leaves of peace
into the night,
laughing
like a couple of kids
violating curfew
while our intellectual selves
went to sleep.

Then we would go back
and find something
to eat,
laughing
like fools.
You made fun
of the American bread
(potato bread)
and I
made fun of your

super crip maneuver
at peeling off the wax
of some fancy cheese
we found
in the refrigerator.
Those
are moments
I shall never
forget.

Nor
will I forget
the delicious shivers
running down my back
as we waited backstage.
The nudity
of your manhood
inches from my face
almost making me forget
the nerves
that previously
devoured me.

Yes,
backstage
we were hot
like tamales.

You, fully naked,
moving your hips
side to side,
my eyes fixed on you –
and you knew it.
You knew it
and loved it.
We both did.
And even though
nothing happened
between us,
we fell in love
with each other's Muses,
each other's art –
the crip spirit
of who we are.

You, Mattie, Mat,
I am honored to know you
and blessed to love you –
my adorable Seal Boy,
my vegetarian T-Rex,
beautiful Freak,
and the most gentle loving Beast
I have ever known.

Decade Of Love
(For Peter.)

You say I am
brutally honest.
And I am,
especially
when it comes
to love.
It is perhaps
that honesty,
what for the last decade
of our lives
has made us love
each other
with sensual
and yet peaceful
love.

We have been friends
and in so many ways;
we have been
lovers.

At times
I have been
a secret
in your life,
and you have been
my salvation, my friend,
my light.

So many times
you have taken
my broken soul
in your arms
and painted hope
on a new canvas,
your version of Maria,
lovingly sketched
by your hand.

And so many times,
you,
like God,
have heard
my prayers.
With your loving hand
you dried my tears
and pulled me
back up.

You have loved me
unconditionally,
even when there was
manhood
bursting behind a zipper;
you've always known
there is
no magic slipper
that can possibly
fit
me.

And yet,
you love me still.
You love me
across thousands of miles
and international lines,
borders we cross
as if they were nothing
because we always feel
so close.

We have rested
on your painted prairies
and hills
and heard the whispers

of windmills
after making love.

One by one
the last ten years have grown
wrinkles of wisdom
between the creases
of passion.
Ten years
is a bite
out of somebody's life
and we
have left
the mark of our teeth
on the forbidden apple
of our story.

You have seen me go
from confused, divorced, scared,
to recently self-proclaimed Goddess,
to the
all-grown-up, sure-of-herself, fearless,
She-Warrior Goddess
I became.
And you watched me
spread my wings
from afar,

witnessing
my every move,
my early attempts
to fly...
my early
poems.

You know
the ins and outs of Maria,
no matter
which version of me
you paint
or what version of you
I write.
You are
one of the many
I love.
You have always
known that.
I am Frida
in every sense
of the word.

In the honor of our Love,
I thank you
and bless
the moment I met you.

I bless
the sound of your voice
and the sound of our laughter
together.
I bless the pencil
and the brush
that make you sketch
and paint
new versions of me...
from the Silent Hills
where we've made love
to the winter snow
that makes me shiver
in your paintings.
I love you
and I say it
with the "brutal" honesty
of true Love.

May the Great Mother
continue to bless
your Muse,
the artist in you,
your inner drummer,
the spirit that made me
fall in love
with you.

For Mark O'Brien

The last day of July
you came into the world
kicking and screaming,
something your body forgot
how to do
one night when polio came
like a silent thief
stealing air from your lungs,
stealing motion from your limbs,
and leaving nothing
but words.

Words came easy for you.
Your words could breathe
and run.
A blank page was a baseball field.
Your poems all played baseball
and ran free
like the child you,
in many ways,
never ceased to be.

I think of you and your poems –
words born from your captivity
into the freedom of your page,
that even then,
never left your side.
They never flew
too far away from your cage.

July came and went,
but your poems stayed –
breathing Berkley nights
and summer breeze,
while I drown
in the open mouth
of a Houston August night
and think
of you.

Dance Into My Thoughts
(For Antoine Hunter.)

You dance into my thoughts
with the ease
of music
you can't hear,
but so clearly feel
with all your soul.

From the minute I knew
I would be meeting you,
I wanted to learn
how to say your name
in sign language
so you could hear me
say "*Antoine*"
with the kind of love
you would immediately
feel,
like you feel the music
that makes you move
in ways
I never will.

I hear the music you dance to,
and you hear the silence
of my feet.

So I asked your interpreter
to teach me your name
in ASL. "A.D.," she signed
as she repeated. "In the deaf world,
he goes by A.D.," she said.

When you walked in
I smiled at you,
signing your name
with my right hand,
and you
dropped down to your knees
like worshiping a Goddess
and hugged me.

We hugged every day –
more than once –
flirting with each other
every chance we got.
I learned
how to sign the word "sexy"
and "hot"
and you

spoke my name,
undressing me with your eyes
before the last "a" in Maria
got silent
between your lips.

And I confess to wanting you
and dreaming
of your masculine chest,
imagining my fingers
teasing the silk
of your brown skin,
so deliciously lusty
to my eyes.

Your male energy
made me thrive
in the abundance
of my own sexuality,
and neither one of us
was shy
or had to explain
why
we felt what we felt.
It just wasn't the time
or the moment
to take things

beyond a hug,
although
we would have loved to
and might have
under different circumstances.

Watching you dance
during a week of rehearsals
inspired me
and touched me.
You hear music
the same way you hear love –
the same way I hear words
when they flow into poems.
It is the Great Muse that moves us
to hear, see and feel,
with senses
that may not know how
otherwise.

I love you.
I love the music in you
and the magic of your body
as it dances
to the sound of notes
your ears can't embrace
but your soul does.

I love Antoine,
the dancer,
the artist,
the friend,
and the *Sexy Male Specimen*
who makes my desires rise
and come to life
every time you dance
into my thoughts.

Generous
(For Lizbeth Ortiz, whose painting,
I Was Generous,
inspired this piece.)

Yes, all of us women
have been
generous –
generous
with the men
we have loved,
with their clumsy hands
and their rough kisses.
We
have been broken
to pieces
and put back together
on the shelf
where again
we found the courage
to love.

We have been
generous –

too generous at times,
and too
forgiving –
always painting
the big picture bigger
and then pulling the trigger
on ourselves.

And God knows
I've too
been generous
more than I should have,
from invented fireworks
and love words
to the
fake orgasms
of my youth.

Yes, us women
are all
about giving,
but eventually
our generosity runs out.
The well of passion dries out
and we reach a point
when,
if a penis talks to us,

it better
be telling
the truth.

Loving You

I have cried for you
in the arms of another –
someone who has loved me
the way I love you.
I have cried over your absence
and your silence,
and I have missed you so much
that oceans and rivers
spilled on my pillow
at night
while holding your name close
and tight between my lips
praying for your return.

I have clawed time with my bare hands
while cursing myself
for loving you
without even knowing you,
and tried to make myself forget
the soft caress of your words
on my page,
the way my poems stretched

and danced
at the very thought
of you.

I have whispered your name
between dreams,
between poems,
without telling a soul.
And then I have told the world
about my pain
without really saying how or why or whom
I love.

I have just called for you
with the energy
of desperate Love,
thinking you have come to me
disguised as a moth,
a butterfly
or a barking dog.

I have found you in everything
I do and love,
even in the arms of a lover
who has loved me, knowing
that I am loving
you.

Tell me. If this is not Love,
what is?
What is love but the nude expression
of the soul...
the merging of two worlds
that found each other,
and loved each other,
knowing
the impossibility
of it all
yet
the eternity of
what is meant to be.

That is who you are to me,
Oh Love of Mine.
Even if I wanted to deny
my love for you,
some things are greater than ourselves.
In matters of the heart,
it is no longer up to us.
I surrender to the pain
and the joy
of loving
you.

About The Author

Maria R. Palacios is a poet, author, spoken word performer, motivational speaker, social change advocate, disability rights activist, and workshop facilitator. Featured on numerous local radio shows and podcasts, nationally syndicated programs, and in many international publications, Maria's impact on the rights of children, women, people with disabilities, and the Hispanic community is as immeasurable as her artistry is undeniable.

Some of Maria's most cherished accomplishments and positions include her participation in efforts that led to the passage of the Americans with Disabilities Act of 1990, being inducted into the Hispanic Women in Leadership Hall of Fame in 1996 and receiving the Hispanic Excellence Award in 1997, being a member of the International Guild of Disabled Artists and Performers since 2009, exploring her personal connection to Frida Kahlo through live performances of her poetry at Houston's annual Frida Fest celebration for seven straight years, participating in the Gulf Coast Poetry Tour (2009), and creating a publishing company (Atahualpa Press) which has produced eight of her own titles to date, as well as two by other artists with disabilities.

Of particular passion to Maria is Sins Invalid, a performance project of artists with disabilities. With this group she has performed since 2007, co-facilitated their Tongue Rhythm Multi-Disciplinary Poetry Workshop in 2008, and is featured in the 2013 documentary, Sins Invalid: An Unashamed Claim to Beauty in the Face of Invisibility. In the artistic world, Maria is known as "The Goddess on Wheels."

palaciosmaria66@gmail.com

www.ingramcontent.com/pod-product-compliance
Lightning Source LLC
Chambersburg PA
CBHW070634160426

43194CB00009B/1455